CONTENTS

"Brant has earned his reputation by consistently delivering some of the most creative and memorable pitches. Now you can learn to do what he does in *The 3-Minute Rule*."   —Paul Buccieri, president, A+E Networks Group

"Having a great idea is just the first step. Getting that idea out in the world so it gets people excited enough to buy in is something Brant Pinvidic has perfected. Now you can learn his foolproof method in *The 3-Minute Rule*."
                —Brad Fuller, partner, Platinum Dunes

"An absolute must-read for anyone who wants to make more effective, memorable presentations."
                —Tony DiSanto, former president of programming, MTV

"*The 3-Minute Rule* teaches an important lesson—one that we could all learn better."   —Jonathan Murray, founder, Bunim/Murray Productions

"If you can take your idea and convey it to others in the simplest form, you'll find success. Brant and his 3-Minute Rule will show you exactly how to do that."   —Jeff Gaspin, former chairman, NBCUniversal Television Entertainment

"I can say without hesitation that Brant is the best I've ever worked with, and *The 3-Minute Rule* is his best work yet."
                —Hank Cohen, former president, MGM Television Entertainment

"*The 3-Minute Rule* is the ultimate guide for communication, not just for pitching, but for life."
                —Thom Sherman, senior executive vice president,
                programming, CBS Entertainment

"Of the thousands of pitches I took during my time as a buyer, Brant's stand out as the most memorable. As he outlines here, he has the ability to make the most complex ideas sound simple and understandable."
                —John Saade, former executive vice president, alternative series,
                specials, and late night, ABC Entertainment

"I often get asked, 'What's the best way to pitch an idea?' Now I can simply say, 'You MUST read *The 3-Minute Rule*, and stick to it.'"

—Jon Sinclair, executive vice president, programming and development, OWN: The Oprah Winfrey Network

"I've personally watched Brant take what is probably the most difficult skill to master and make it look simple and easy. *The 3-Minute Rule* will do the same for you."

—Paraag Marathe, president, 49ers Enterprises, and executive vice president, Football Operations

"It is rare that you get a business book this fun to read and this practical and insightful. *The 3-Minute Rule* is a must for anyone looking to pitch or present anything to anyone." —Bill Walshe, CEO, Viceroy Hotel Group

"Brant helps people understand that there have been massive technology shifts in how we communicate. To get people to hear what you have to say is a real art form in communication. I think Brant has given this more thought and has more ideas on how to make communication dramatically more effective than the vast majority of experts I've seen in the field."

—David Weild IV, former vice chairman, NASDAQ

"After one read of this book plus three short minutes, I am a better advocate when I pitch my cases and ideas for settlement, or advocate to the decision makers in my world—a judge, a jury, or even opposing counsel."

—Robin Sax, former California state prosecutor, Los Angeles

"You can have the best idea in the world, but if you can't pitch it, then what's the use? *The 3-Minute Rule* gives you the skill and the confidence you need to be pitch-perfect." —Patrick Drake, cofounder, HelloFresh

"It's about more than just being brief. *The 3-Minute Rule* is about building value clearly and concisely in any pitch or presentation."

—Sylvie di Giusto, CSP, keynote speaker, and past president, National Speakers Association, New York City

"*The 3-Minute Rule* absolutely blew me away, but I wasn't surprised. I've watched Brant pitch since he first came to LA. I've always thought his ability to communicate an idea in a clear, concise, compelling way was unique, and now it looks like he's figured out how to teach that secret to the rest of us." —Matt Walden, principal, The Make Good Group

"I would not make a pitch today without *The 3-Minute Rule* by my side."

—Brian Cristiano, CEO, BOLD Worldwide

"*The 3-Minute Rule* will change the way you look at communicating, both personally and professionally."

—Ben Nemtin, coauthor of *What Do You Want to Do Before You Die?*

"Brant has built a large fan base from our highly skeptical and critical audience; me included! *The 3-Minute Rule* captures Brant's personality and practical life lessons in an entertaining way. A must-read if you plan to raise capital." —Nico P. Pronk, president and CEO, Noble Capital Markets

"It's so important for anyone in business, it should be called *The 3-Minute Law*." —Hugh Ruthven, former director of marketing, McDonald's

"One of the the most important skills that can positively impact your career is being able to present your ideas to others in a succinct and understandable way. Brant is one of the authorities for those wanting to learn how to make this skill their own."

—Josh Scheinfeld, founder and managing member, Lincoln Park Capital

THE
3-MINUTE
RULE

THE
3-MINUTE
RULE

Say Less to Get More
from Any Pitch or Presentation

BRANT PINVIDIC

Portfolio | Penguin

PORTFOLIO/PENGUIN
An imprint of Penguin Random House LLC
penguinrandomhouse.com

Most Portfolio books are available at a discount when purchased in quantity for
sales promotions or corporate use. Special editions, which include personalized covers,
excerpts, and corporate imprints, can be created when purchased in large quantities. For more
information, please call (212) 572-2232 or e-mail specialmarkets@penguinrandomhouse.com.
Your local bookstore can also assist with discounted bulk purchases using the
Penguin Random House corporate Business-to-Business program. For assistance in
locating a participating retailer, e-mail B2B@penguinrandomhouse.com.

LIBRARY OF CONGRESS CATALOGING-IN-PUBLICATION DATA
Names: Pinvidic, Brant, author.
Title: The 3-minute rule: say less to get more from any pitch or
presentation / Brant Pinvidic.
Description: [New York] : Portfolio/Penguin [2019] | Includes index.
Identifiers: LCCN 2019022702 (print) | LCCN 2019022703 (ebook) |
ISBN 9780525540724 (hardcover) | ISBN 9780525540731 (ebook)
Subjects: LCSH: Business presentations. | Business communication. |
Entrepreneurship. | Success in business.
Classification: LCC HF5718.22.P57 2019 (print) |
LCC HF5718.22 (ebook) | DDC 658.4/5—dc23
LC record available at https://lccn.loc.gov/2019022702
LC ebook record available at https://lccn.loc.gov/2019022703

Printed in Canada
1 3 5 7 9 10 8 6 4 2

Book design by Gretchen Achilles

For my wife, Juliana. You've been through all of it.
My neural pathways are accustomed to your inputs.

And Kahless, Briana, and Braden.
The three better versions of me to be.

Albert the Turkey: We miss you.

INTRODUCTION

Every time you make a pitch, presentation, or proposal to try to influence anyone to do anything, your audience's first impression will be fully formed in less than three minutes. That yes or no is already in their heads. It's not your fault. That's just how people are.

For the last two decades the human attention span has been steadily decreasing. Now, a recent Microsoft study puts the average human attention span at 8.2 seconds.

A goldfish is at 9 seconds.

It's not that we're all dumbed-down, mindless, distracted zombies (although if you have teenagers, you might disagree), it's actually just the opposite.

In fact, people today focus more *intensely* and *efficiently*. The proliferation of technology and the ability to get unlimited information instantly have created hypersavvy consumers. They have zero tolerance for long-winded explanations, exhaustive chatter, or linguistic sales tactics. They will tune you out in an 8.2-second instant.

Audiences today simply want information. They want it quick, clear, and concise.

It doesn't matter if you're presenting to the board of directors of a major research hospital or the PTA at the local high school. This reality will be smacking you right in the face. I'm betting you've already been feeling it.

I know I have. We're all in the same boat.

To succeed, you must be able to capture and hold your audience's attention with only the quality and flow of your information, long enough to take them through that initial decision-making process. They must *conceptualize* your idea, *contextualize* how it will benefit them, and then *actualize* it with potential engagement or further interest.

You have about three minutes.

And so do I.

A typical introduction to a business book can be more than fourteen pages long. Yet most readers decide if they are going to read a new book in the first six pages or less. Which, no surprise, takes about three minutes to read.

So before we get to anything else, the only thing that matters is that I get you enthusiastic enough to read past these first six pages. Here we go:

This book is a step-by-step guide that will show you how to simplify your message by strategically condensing your business, product, or service down to the most valuable and compelling elements. Then, using high-level Hollywood storytelling techniques, you'll learn to convey those elements in a concise and convincing fashion.

This system is based on the core principles behind the 3-Minute Rule:

Everything of value about your company, idea, product, or service can and must be conveyed clearly, concisely, and accurately in three minutes or less. In the first three minutes, you need to vividly illustrate the most valuable elements of your proposal, capture and maintain your audience's attention, and—most important—create engagement.

By following this rule, you will be able to **Say Less and Get More** from every pitch or presentation.

I'm not talking about an "elevator pitch." Serious meetings, real business, and effective communication take longer and require more fine-tuning than blurting out a few catchy phrases in an elevator.

This is about delivering your most valuable information in the most compelling way to ensure further engagement. Three minutes is not just a time frame to condense your information; it's based on the science of **approach motivation**, the study of why consumers are driven to engage. The science says, if you can maintain their *focus,* you can *create their desire.* You need three minutes.

Simplicity is power

Clarity is compelling

Information is value

The key is to separate everything you ***want*** to say from just what ***needs*** to be said.

This book will show you *exactly* how to do that.

The process for creating and delivering the most effective and impactful three minutes is a two-step system, keeping in mind that the rest of the book is going to explain and flesh out each of these concepts:

Step one: Simplify and condense information to only the most compelling, valuable, and *necessary* elements. Create a point-by-point path that guides the audience through this information, building to the desired conclusion.

Step two: Connect these elements with entertaining and narrative story devices that capture and maintain the audience's attention and expand it for the full three minutes. Focus the audience's attention in order to create desire for your objective.

By using these two steps as detailed throughout the book, you'll be able to deliver the most powerful and effective version of your message and ensure that what you **need** to say gets heard and understood.

Throughout, you'll discover how to

- use surefire Hollywood storytelling techniques to transform a basic pitch into a highly efficient and engaging story;
- deliver information in digestible pieces and lead your audience to draw the right conclusions;
- make the first three minutes the most impactful and effective moments of your presentation so you earn the chance to go further; and
- weave your elements into an entertaining story so that you're saying less and delivering more.

Whether you're a consultant, account executive, fast-food restaurant manager, personal trainer, or general contractor, you'll be able to use the guiding principles in this book to convey your ideas to others in the most efficient and effective way possible. You'll be able to use it in all facets of your life.

And you'll be able to do it fast.

The forthcoming chapters lay out the four-step **WHAC** process, a powerful guide that helps you identify, evaluate, and order the most important elements of your presentation. By answering the four WHAC questions ("**W**hat is it? **H**ow does it work? **A**re You Sure? **C**an you do it?"), you will weave your most crucial points into a compelling narrative structure and discover how to use the power of storytelling in any setting and at any level.

We're going to start with breaking down your pitch or presentation into a bullet point format, then expand those points into core **statements of value**. We'll then connect them using some of the most effective and powerful Hollywood storytelling techniques. You'll follow along as we craft a full 3-Minute pitch from scratch. I'll even show you exactly how to effectively open and close any pitch, presentation, or meeting.

Along the way you'll meet Vince McMahon, Jon Bon Jovi, Jimmy Fallon, Cameron Diaz, dozens of fluffy bunny rabbits, plumbers, oil prospectors, people setting up Airbnbs for horses, and more than one befuddled CEO; learn what a Butt Funnel is; discover that Freebird isn't just a song; attend a forty-three-person decision-making meeting; take the fire alarm and telephone tests; come to love Post-it notes and loathe PowerPoint; and find the **hook** and the **edge** of your story.

This book comes out of my two decades of experience as a Hollywood producer and top-level C-suite coach and presentation consultant.

I've been involved in nearly ten thousand pitches, and by

using this system I've sold more than three hundred TV and movie projects to more than forty different TV networks and distributors. In three minutes each, I've sold TV shows, like *Extreme Makeover: Weight Loss Edition* and *Bar Rescue*, and have grossed nearly a billion dollars in revenue.

But my methods don't just work for Hollywood: Over the last five years, I've dedicated my life to helping people like you by teaching the art of pitching, presenting, and selling, no matter what they're trying to sell. I've successfully taught these principles to hundreds, from Fortune 100 CEOs to PTA presidents. These methods have helped plumbers sell home restoration systems, lawyers win cases, and oil drillers sell stock.

It's easier than you fear and takes less work than you're doing now. You will be saying less, and I promise you, you'll be getting much, much more.

I could go on for another dozen pages about what the book will do for you and how it's going to do it. But it wouldn't help. You've most likely already decided if you're going to read further. That's why the first three minutes of any pitch, presentation, proposal, or book intro are so crucial.

Never lose someone in the first three minutes again.

Let's get started.

CHAPTER 1

THE 3-MINUTE RULE

Let's begin by dispelling some of the most common misconceptions about the pitching and presenting process. This foundation of understanding will help you build your most effective first three minutes.

Misconception #1—Your presentation needs flair, pageantry, and creative language to cut through the clutter and get noticed.

It's the exact opposite.

When I help people with their presentations, the first question I ask is, "With all these slides and all this information and all the jokes and all the quotes from famous people, what are you trying to do with this pitch or presentation?"

The response is usually about their final objective and involves their ultimate goal of, say, increasing sales to a certain level to sell the company.

I tell them to think smaller and simplify.

They give me a monthly sales goal.

"Smaller and simpler!"

This dance goes on until they are out of answers. This exercise is crucial to understanding the fundamental principle behind influencing anyone to do anything.

The answer, in the simplest terms: "You are trying to convey information effectively."

If you can get others to understand your information the way you do, all of your other goals and objectives will be the happy by-product.

If people understand the value of your product like you do, you'll sell more. If your organization understands your proposal the way you do, they will vote in your favor.

The theory behind this process is something you can apply to all aspects of your life.

Here it is:

Success in life and business is dictated by your ability to convey your information to others so they understand it the way you do.

If you do that well, you can sell. If you do that well, you can market. You could even write a book.

If you give up all your preconceptions about language, tactics, phrasing, or technique and focus only on the value of your information and the process of translating that information in a way that your audience will understand, I promise you'll succeed.

The 3-Minute Rule will guide you step by step to take your most compelling and valuable information and weave it into an engaging story that will lead your audience where you want them to go.

Misconception #2—My business, product, or service is too complicated to explain in three minutes. I have too much to say.

Nearly all the company leaders and CEOs I work with tell me something like, "I just cannot condense my presentation into anything less than ten minutes. There is just too much information."

I tell them they're wrong.

Three minutes is not only a benchmark for condensing the valuable elements of a proposal and streamlining a presentation, it also serves to engage an audience to where they begin their decision-making process. If you can't distill your ideas down to three minutes or less, they will begin to make a decision without all the pertinent information. You definitely do not want your audience doing that.

In every TV show, the conflict in each scene is edited to resolve at almost exactly the three-minute mark. *Shark Tank*, for example, uses this decision marker in nearly every episode. From the time they introduce an entrepreneur to the time one of the Sharks says "I'm out," it is almost always three minutes.

I pitch more than forty TV shows a year, and every one of my sales tapes is now almost exactly three minutes. Within the first three minutes of any presentation or pitch, the audience will process the basic elements of your offering, start to place value on that offering, and determine their likelihood to continue further with meaningful engagement.

That's why it's so important to control that narrative and guide the audience through each facet of a presentation.

It's also vital to know whom you're actually speaking to.

Sometimes there is a single decision-maker to convince, but more often than not there is another layer to get through. They are going to have to convince someone else, and that person has someone else to convince, and so on. Your pitch is most likely going to be run around the block by others when you're not even there.

We'll see later how to make your message so clear that it survives this corporate game of telephone. But first, let me tell you about one of the most daunting audiences I ever had to convince.

DECISION BY COMMITTEE

One time a couple of years ago, I was waiting in the lobby of the National Geographic building in Washington, DC, when the network president's secretary came to greet me. "Howard would like you to come join this meeting for a minute," she said.

Since I was just there to take Howard to lunch, I wasn't prepared for any meeting.

Howard was my friend, and he had just taken over as president of the National Geographic Channel. He had mentioned that earlier that morning he would be having his company-wide green light meeting. The green light meeting is where the network makes the final decisions on which shows get made and which shows die right there. I had a show that I sold to Nat Geo as a pilot that I knew they were discussing in that meeting. Since Howard was the president, and I knew that he loved the show, I was expecting our lunch date to be a celebratory meal.

Howard greeted me outside the meeting room door.

"Brant, we were just talking about your show and I was having a tough time explaining it as well as you do, and there were a bunch of questions, so since I knew you were downstairs, I thought it was better to have you come up."

This was highly irregular. He was bringing me into the network green light meeting. Producers never sat in on these meetings. Ever.

But that wasn't the weirdest part.

There were forty-three people in this meeting sitting around a huge conference table. Really. Forty-three. During the inevitable lulls, I amused myself by counting them.

I couldn't believe how many people were at that table! I've heard that insiders used to say that IBM stood for Incredibly Big Meetings, and if any of you ever worked there, please let me know if they ever made it to forty-three.

The questions started. What surprised me was how confused and misinformed (and grumpy) the others at this meeting seemed to be. Howard was the president of the network, and I knew he understood and was excited about the show. But when he had relayed it, there was obviously something lost in translation.

There were times it felt like people in that room were actively trying to find a way to say something negative. I could feel the show slipping away as the discussion kept getting longer. Luckily, using the methods that eventually became the 3-Minute Rule, I gave the pitch again.

That ended the conversation. We got a six-episode order.

I was quickly ushered out of the room so they could discuss—or, more accurately, pick apart and destroy—the pitch for the next show whose producer didn't happen to be in the lobby.

I walked away with two crucial realizations from that meeting:

First, as mentioned previously, the size! I'd never seen a meeting with forty-three people trying to make a decision on something.

There were men and women from marketing. From scheduling. From finance. From legal. From HR. There were principals and deputies and deputies to the deputies. Every one of them had an opinion on the creative merits or the viability of the show.

It was stunning.

The number of questions and second-guessing was terrifying. I can only imagine what it would have been like if I wasn't there to correct all that misinformation.

My heart sank when I realized that this was going to happen in every green light meeting for every show I developed.

I tell this story in my speeches, and when I describe this meeting, I always hear the same audible groan of recognition (in any country and any language). What the TV world moved to, and now it's obvious that every industry has moved to, is the concept of **decision by committee**.

The conference room has become a war room.

The second realization this meeting gave me was that all the work I put into pitching and prepping Howard, the president of the network, wasn't enough. He had to take what I had pitched him and then turn around and pitch it to multiple people multiple times. No wonder things got lost in translation. If I couldn't be in every meeting, who was going to be there to champion the idea?

It was clear this was the cause of a disturbing trend I'd been noticing. I'd have such positive and optimistic vibes and conversations with the buyers going *into* the green light meeting, but get blindsided by a pass coming *out* of the meeting. Many times the top executive was just as surprised as I was that the show didn't get the support we all expected.

I knew I had to find a way to combat this insidious decision-by-committee phenomenon. I built every pitch from that moment on with the idea that someone was going to have to share it with someone else. Even if they were the decision-maker, there is always someone else they are going to relay it to.

Always be aware: **It's not just who you pitch to, it's who they have to pitch to, that matters**.

No matter how much beautifully crafted material you are able to lay out directly, and regardless of how long you immerse someone in the depths of your proposal, they are going to have to summarize and relay your pitch to someone else.

Let's say you spent an entire hour presenting to someone and it results in what you consider to be the absolute best possible meeting in history. This person just absorbed an entire hour of your information. Let's say they completely understand it, and they really love it.

Now when they come across someone else in their life and that person asks them, "Why did you like that presentation?" I'll let you guess how long it takes them to answer that question and relay everything of value they retained.

Yes, three minutes. You just had the greatest hour-long meeting in history . . . but three minutes is about all you're getting back.

When you are done reading this book, I hope you're going to want to share it with all your friends (as many as possible), and they'll ask, "What is the book about? Why should I read it?"

You will instinctively condense this entire book into a three-minutes-or-less explanation. I spent years developing these ideas and eighteen months writing this book, and you'll tell people everything about it in less than three minutes.

It's just how we instinctively process and relay information.

Now, tell me all about one of your favorite two-hour movies, or the last four-hundred-page book you read. You'll see. Three minutes is all you need.

You'll find that no matter the subject or how much information someone takes in, they're going to use what I call the **rationalization story** to explain it to themselves and to others.

You might find this frustrating, but this is a good thing. Like I said earlier, three minutes is not just timing for which you condense your information. There's a lot of science behind it.

THE RATIONALIZATION STORY

The two most important factors to consider when building any presentation or proposal are **knowledge** and **rationalization**:

1. What **knowledge** does my audience already possess? (We'll get to this a little later.)
2. How will they **rationalize** the decision to "buy in" to my proposal?

Simply put, humans are the only species that has the power to rationalize. Every other creature uses instinct and knowledge to make decisions, where humans use the ability to rationalize. It's a remarkable and powerful emotional ability. And it's the basis and foundation for every decision we make.

Everything you ever decide or have to do must be rationalized in your head to yourself. It's the "why" behind everything we do. More important, it's the accepted, understood "why" that we believe and we can embrace and live with.

The ability to rationalize is so powerful, it drives everything from our mundane day-to-day decisions to why we do horrible things to each other. We are so programmed to rationalize that we can come up with an acceptable rationalization for almost any behavior. Whether it's what toothpaste to use or whether to commit murder, that decision will be rationalized and accepted by the human brain.

This is where things get interesting. When you rationalize any decision, your mind naturally categorizes all of the elements of that decision and relays them back to you in the most effective and persuasive way to make you "justify" the decision.

Let's do a little self-assessment.

I want you to answer a simple question: Why do you drive the car you drive?

Answer this in one sentence. Got the answer?

"I like it." Or "It was a good deal." Or "I've always had that model."

Now go one step further. Explain to yourself why you chose that car and why you drive that car. For each answer, ask why. Go a few layers deep.

"It was a good deal and it gets good mileage and it doesn't break down and I never worry about it."

You are now justifying and rationalizing your decision. You will justify your feelings and desires and how they came to be. If you keep asking and answering why in your head, you'll clearly see the rationale for the decision.

Now I want you to play that back in your head and picture yourself saying it out loud.

This is important.

You're going to hear something remarkable.

Your mind has naturally placed the most valuable factors in that decision up front and in a specific order. To you, the decision of why you bought and drive that car is explained perfectly. You begin with the most valuable summarizing statement, then the more whys you ask, you reveal the layers, arranged in importance, that rationalize those statements.

You will break down your reason for any decision using simple declarative sentences and phrases. To yourself, you use just the basic and simple version of even the most complex elements. You don't do long explanations.

It's amazing. Try it again.

Why do you live in your city? Or why do you have the job that you have? Or why did you get married or divorced? What movie are you going to go see this weekend and why?

Go a few layers deep on the why questions, answering them in short, simple sentences. These are called **statements of value**. They represent what's important to you, and your brain naturally organizes them in order to build your story.

That is the **rationalization story.**

That story is the collection of the most valuable elements placed together so you can understand your actions, your feelings, and your desires. If you just booked a vacation, you will have used the rationalization story, without thinking about it, to decide where to go, where to stay, how much to spend, and what to pack. You use a story like that for every decision in your life.

That story is precise. That story is succinct. That story says only what needs to be said. That story is the clearest, most efficient way to convey the information to yourself.

If you are attempting to convince anyone of anything, that rationalization story is what they will use to make their decision. Even if you spend three hours pitching every single detail, they will ultimately rationalize their decision using a simple story and collection of statements, guaranteed to be less than three minutes long.

Imagine if your pitch were built on the rationalization story that your audience would use to say yes to your proposal.

What you're going to learn in these next chapters is how to build that rationalization story for your audience, based solely on your information. I'll show you how to identify the most valuable elements of your proposal and then take those elements and weave them together in a way that mimics that rationalization story.

THE FIRST STEP

Much of what you're about to read and start to practice may initially feel counterintuitive. Trust me, that's good.

You can say less and get more.

In 1929 Joe Kennedy said that the shoeshine boy was giving him stock tips and that's when he knew it was time to get out of the market. It's always a good idea to zig when everyone is zagging.

In a world crowded by marketing and messaging, everyone seems to be yelling louder and louder. You don't want to try to outshout them. It feels like everyone is trying to say more, say it more often, and make it sound bigger and better. You can work smarter, not harder. Speak more softly and get heard.

I began to build every TV pitch (or any other pitch) with that idea—to say less and get more. It forced me to be more efficient and deliberate. It was stunning how effective that became. Three minutes was the magic number.

As we progress through the book, you'll be able to identify this pattern in anything you want to present. You'll carry it across all your pitches or marketing or sales needs. It will become part of how you look at conveying information to others.

Over the past years I dedicated my life to developing this system and being able to help people pitch and present at the highest level. I get calls from CEOs and business leaders from across the country, and I've been able to work with some of the most amazing people, many of whom you'll meet in coming chapters. Sometimes it felt surreal explaining to the CEO of a multibillion-dollar company how to simplify their message. All the millions of dollars they spent on customer research and investor relations wasn't helping them to say less and get more.

CHAPTER 2

THE BULLETS

Just over a decade ago, I was blindly struggling as a TV development executive at an emerging production company. My job was to take the germ of an idea and somehow get it on TV. I had to not only create and develop the premise for the show but also convince the network executives to buy it, pay to make it, and then put it on their channel.

Every day was a battle trying to get the head of this or that TV network to see the value in the show I had just created. The pitch process was intense and difficult. But it was all I knew. A big part of the job was watching good ideas die because the network "didn't get it."

At the time, taking a show from the idea stage through the pitch stage was about a ninety-day process. The idea usually only took two or three days to formulate, but it would take us weeks to prepare all the detailed written and graphic material, film and edit a so-called sizzle tape, and set and deliver all the pitches. Each pitch would cost us an average of $30,000 to take to market.

We averaged about one sale for every ten pitches. In television, that was a solid average.

One particular show changed my entire career. It led me to develop the 3-Minute Rule, and it's why you're reading this book.

GETTING EXTREME

My production team had spent three weeks in our cramped LA conference room, shouting in circles about how to best pitch this show. Three weeks and we hadn't even started to craft the pitch deck or film the sales tape because we didn't know how to pitch it. We all knew it was a great idea. We just couldn't figure out how to explain it to anybody else.

It's not that we all became stupid at once. We were just drowning in too many thoughts and too much information.

Part of our issue was that the show we were thinking of was wildly complicated, probably way too expensive, had never been done before, and would take five times longer to produce than any other television show we had ever made.

But it was a great idea!

The six of us in the room—with dozens of years of TV experience—saw the beauty of this idea and how it all worked. In that room all the elements and ideas flowed in harmony and added up to a hit show. When it was just us, it was perfect.

But as soon as we'd bring anyone else into the room, it all turned into a jumbled mess. Each meeting would careen off onto another tangent and crash into confusion. This was unbelievably frustrating. My team was losing focus and enthusiasm, and I was losing them. I had no idea how to make this better.

At the time we were an up-and-coming production company. Our claim to fame was that we were the producers of *The Biggest Loser*. This was a hit NBC prime-time television series airing around the world. It was the first weight loss TV show, and with its overwhelming success, we were scrambling to come up with more shows about weight loss. (In Hollywood, when one show's a hit, others like it are sure to follow.)

We needed to crack the next evolution of this format before somebody else did.

I knew in this conference room that we had the next big hit. I could see it crystal clear in my head. I just couldn't explain it.

Slumped in my chair in that conference room, the walls closing in, I was as frustrated as I've ever been in my life. I just couldn't get it. If I weren't Canadian, I would've been shouting and snipping at my assistants. Instead I just seethed. I ate way too much cold pizza and got way too little sleep.

It was at this moment that I discovered the very core of what later became the 3-Minute Rule and the entire foundation of everything I speak, teach, and coach today. That moment is burned into my memory.

COULD IT BE THAT SIMPLE?

I want to try to illustrate how messy and overloaded our original pitch for this show really was. It's difficult because in hindsight I see it so simply and clearly that I have a hard time replicating the convoluted way it looked twelve years ago.

But here is my attempt:

The idea for the next great weight loss show involves looking at the casting tapes from *The Biggest Loser*, taking people who were too big to compete on the show, and, instead of making them compete to lose weight by tempting them with food and exercise challenges, letting them work through the struggles on their own.

We will help them when they need guidance, but it is ultimately up to them. Lasting weight loss takes time, so we'll actually be filming them the entire time they lose weight. Since it will take a long time to film, we'll have to condense a lot of time into little segments so you can see all of the progress in one hour. We won't have them all in a house together, so all their stories are going to be separate, and they won't know each other or work with each other. There will be no teams, no rivalries, no getting voted off the island.

It will just be their individual stories, told from their perspectives. Note that if they aren't losing weight in a competitive situation they won't lose weight as quickly, and since these people are so big, the change will be more gradual. Since it would be too slow to carry over a series of episodes, and the audience would get bored, each episode will be devoted to one individual's story of personal transformation—and the following week's episode will focus on a different person. There will be no connection from one episode to the next, nothing to have to remember from week to week.

There were another five paragraphs about how we would actually film and edit the show and rotate crews to save cost over the year. And how we would hire one trainer for the year to travel to a different contestant each week, and how we would need to bring in off-camera trainers to monitor the contestants because someone would need to babysit them or they wouldn't lose weight. I also had to describe how these contestants would be living in their own homes and not on a ranch or in a "reality house," so there were things we would need to do with their jobs and lives to make sure we could film the important aspects all year long.

Are you unimpressed and way confused? Good. It was even worse in real time.

When we ran our mock pitch meetings, this explanation would take about eighteen minutes. I felt like I said everything I wanted to say and had relayed all the relevant information, but nobody could possibly stay interested or focused for that long. Most times I'd get interrupted in the middle with questions about parts of the show I hadn't had a chance to explain yet.

I was dreading the idea of getting in the room with network presidents on this show.

The network pitch room is a cold, ruthless, unforgiving setting with a very difficult audience. Meetings start with smiles that last about ten seconds. If you've ever watched *Shark Tank*, that no-nonsense attitude and curt style was patterned after a TV network pitch. If I couldn't win over employees in my own company, how was I going to win over John Saade or Andrea Wong at ABC?

I actually ached to just give up. I'd done that with hundreds of ideas in the past. I would pitch the show around internally and if people didn't "get it," we'd just move on. I have no problem with people disagreeing with the viability of an idea or thinking it won't sell. But in this case, they were judging it without actually understanding it. It was making me crazy.

Luckily for me, I didn't give up. In a moment of pure frustration, I decided to try again with a completely clean slate.

biggest contestants	jogging	one year	start fat
sweat	remote cameras	end thin	compassion
thin dreams	life saving	trainers	grueling
obese	single episodes	trans- formation	diets
exercise	weight- lifting	carb counting	cinema verité

So I returned to our large development conference room and asked the team to write down every statement that described the show on individual Post-it notes in blue Sharpie and then stick them on the wall. At the end of the exercise we had at least a hundred on the wall, so many that it looked like a vast yellow flag with graffiti on it.

Each tiny Post-it could only fit a word or two because we needed to print large enough to read them from across the room. So the words or phrases were originally meant to just be placeholders

And more . . .

Our goal was to arrange these bullet points in an order that made sense and that anyone could follow. But we were continually arguing because each Post-it note idea would spur the room of voluble TV producers into yelling out the details—often all at once. They ended up circling endlessly, chasing their own tails.

I tuned out the yelling in the room and focused on the words on the wall. They overwhelmed me. The wall was filled with everything I *wanted* to say, but I had to find just what *needed* to be said.

One by one, I began to eliminate the words that weren't necessary to the core concept of the show. Eventually I found myself with just seven Post-it notes in the far corner of the wall.

It was like cracking a code, or seeing the solution to a puzzle appear. For the first time, I saw *how* to explain this idea appear before me with perfect clarity.

I stood up and yelled out the door to my assistant: "Jimmy! Get me John Saade at ABC."

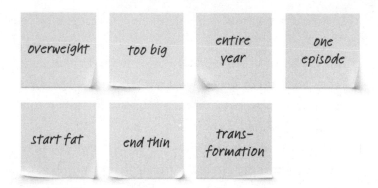

Everyone in the room stared at me wondering what on earth I was doing.

Jimmy yelled back, "I've got John."

I hit the speaker button.

"Brant, you're on with John."

"Hey, Brant, what's up?"

"Hey, John, I have something spectacular. I've been working on it for months and I just cracked it. I have to pitch it to you *today*, right now. Can I come over?"

The room was silent because everyone was holding their breath.

This was not something I'd ever said to the head of a network. I'm guessing he might never have been asked to take a meeting like that.

"I'm a little slammed right now, can we do it next week?" he asked.

"John, I promise it won't take more than five minutes and you'll get it, and I'm telling you, it's worth it."

Again, silence.

"Let me know when you're here. I'll give my office a heads-up."

"I'll be there in thirty minutes."

After a long, stunned silence, my head of development said, "What are you going to do? What are you going to say? We're not even close to ready."

"We are way past ready," I replied. "We have overcooked this. We've been trying way too hard. I just need to get him to see what we see." I pointed to the board of Post-its. He had no clue what the hell I was talking about. But I did.

We had made a collection of some of the people who never made it onto *The Biggest Loser* because they were just so overweight. We had a DVD made of them puffing and straining and failing all the preliminary tests we had devised for contestants on that show.

Our head of production came out to the hall and asked me what I was thinking. He reiterated that we were not ready and that the DVD was just a "mood and emotion tape" that didn't explain anything about how the show would work or what the show even was. He said, "You're going over there with nothing? No paper, no PowerPoint, no budget, no outline, no logo, no episode breakdown. What are you going to even say?"

I asked him to trust me. Five minutes after I hung up the phone with John, I was driving up the 405 freeway toward ABC.

I had to wait in the lobby for over an hour while John took other scheduled meetings.

John looked at me skeptically through his round glasses.

Unlike the typically chatty network people, John was always quiet and purposeful.

"Five minutes" was the first thing he said.

I dropped the DVD on his desk and pointed to it. I uttered nine sentences:

We take overweight people too big for *The Biggest Loser*.

We follow them for one entire year while they lose weight.

We edit that entire year of weight loss into one single episode.

They start out fat and by the end of one hour they are thin.

We film them all at the same time, but each person gets their own episode.

It will be the biggest transformation ever seen on television, every single week.

If you buy this show today, you can't have it on the air for eighteen months.

You may not even have this job by the time it premieres.

But you can show your boss this DVD and say, "I don't know what to do with this, but it's big, and you are seeing it first."

It took a little over a minute.

Crucially, I didn't try to explain every aspect of the show

to John. He knew as much or more about television production than I did. I cut right to the heart of what was important.

We stood there in silence for a few moments.

John reached out and grabbed the DVD off his desk. He looked at me expressionlessly.

"How can you afford to follow the contestants for an entire year?"

"We rotate crews and use remote cameras in their houses," I said.

He twirled the DVD in his fingers, I could see the gears in his head spinning.

"So if you have an entire year of weight loss in one episode, we're talking about hundreds of pounds?"

"We're talking three hundred pounds or more. In one episode of television."

I could see him piecing it all together.

"Can you actually pull it off?"

"Yes, we have the entire production system, calendar, and budget already laid out."

I think he almost smiled. "It's very interesting."

"Watch the DVD, let me know what you want to do," I said as I walked out of the room with more than a minute to spare.

One hour later my phone rang. "John Saade from ABC, line one," Jimmy yelled.

Everyone scurried out of their offices to crowd around my desk. I put John on speaker.

"Hey, John, what's up?"

"Can you do this show for less than $1 million an episode?"

"Depends on how many episodes you order," I said.

"How many do you need to hit that number?"

"I need ten," I said, making it up on the spot.

"OK, you'll have an offer this afternoon. Don't pitch it anywhere else."

"OK, you got it," I said, trying to keep my bulging heart and cracking voice under control.

"Great job, great pitch. You bring stuff like this to me anytime."

"OK, bye," I squeaked.

The room erupted. Think Mount Vesuvius. Think Krakatoa.

This was the biggest moment of my career. It made our company.

The show premiered eighteen months later in 2011 on ABC as *Extreme Makeover: Weight Loss Edition* and was one of the highest-rated summer reality series in that network's history. The show ran for five seasons and more than fifty episodes. We saved countless lives and gave morbidly obese people hope and the ability to do things they couldn't before, like picking up their children, walking a daughter down the aisle, and other life-changing moments that only became possible after they lost three hundred pounds.

The show generated hundreds of millions of dollars in revenue and spawned versions in more than fifty countries. To this day it's still my proudest television accomplishment.

All this from a pitch that lasted less than three minutes. I said only what was needed, not everything I wanted to say. I let the idea do all the work.

Those Post-it notes on the wall showed me the path.

WHAT I WAS DOING WRONG

Before I had my epiphany, I was trying too hard. Over the previous few years, I had gotten inside my head and too tangled up with how things were done in the TV producing world. I wanted to explain it all. I wanted to show how much I knew, how much work I had done, how smart I was.

I was trying to sell instead of conveying information. I wasn't letting the ideas do the work. I wasn't telling a story.

After that pitch for *Extreme Weight Loss*, things changed in my office. We went through a lot of Post-it notes (I should have invested in 3M). As more ideas came in through our development process, we started breaking them down in similar fashion into single words and phrases. It almost became a game where we'd go around the table and each member of my team would post a word or phrase related to the show. You'd hear the oohs and aahs and "good one" as we filled the board.

The results were amazing. I sold more TV shows. A lot more TV shows.

Not only were more of the shows we pitched getting sold, I was able to pitch more ideas. Instead of ninety days to get an idea pitched out to networks, I was doing it in less than thirty. Instead of spending an average of $30,000 for a pitch tape and material, we were averaging less than $10,000.

I was filming less, editing less, designing less, working less, and getting *way, way, way* more. My reputation for having the best pitches in the industry was growing rapidly.

I couldn't wait to get in the room with the network presidents. The process was invigorating.

Since that day I've sold more than three hundred TV projects and nearly fifty TV series. These shows have generated nearly a billion dollars in revenue and helped me become one of the industry's most recognized and acclaimed pitchmen and sales executives.

I never broke my 3-Minute Rule. Not once.

When you look back at my *Extreme Weight Loss* pitch, you can see how the simple bullet points helped form the framework of the entire pitch.

- We find **overweight people** who are too big for *The Biggest Loser.*
- We follow them for an **entire year** while they lose weight.
- We edit that entire year of weight loss into **one episode**.
- They **start out fat** and by the end of the hour they **are thin**.
- We film all of them at the same time, then they each get their **own episode**.
- It will be biggest **transformation** ever on television, every single week.

Your first step is to create a master list of all the bullet points you can come up with that describe what you do or what you want to present. Once you have the master list, I'll show you how to identify your most valuable bullet points and then connect them all with simple declarative sentences that will capture and hold your audience's attention . . . for a full three minutes.

Start by asking yourself a few simple questions and use only one- or two-word phrases. Use Post-it notes or index cards and a marker and write down your answers.

What do you do?

What do you do well?

Or:

What is it?

Why is it good?

If you were asking for a raise at work, your questions might be: Why do you deserve it? Why are you worth it?

Make these questions fit your offering. What do you want someone to do or buy? Why should they do it or buy it? What's in it for them? The questions are asking you to bullet-point the concept, how it works, and why it's good. Tell me in single words or phrases everything relevant about your business, product, or service. Don't edit yourself; we'll get to that part soon enough.

When you think you've got them all, go get a cup of coffee or a glass of water. Come back and write down more. The key to this exercise is volume (thirty minimum). The more you write, the easier it will be to sort them later.

You'll be stunned at how much information your list will contain.

Let me show you something.

Here are thirty-one bullet points from a client of mine whose story you'll hear about in a later chapter.

See how much you can gather about his company by just these words and phrases in no particular order:

- Plumbing company
- Burbank, CA
- Re-piping homes
- PEX pipes
- Water problems
- Replace pipes
- Only re-piping
- Not major renovation
- Tiny holes
- No mess
- Old homes
- Every faucet
- National call center
- Old pipes stay
- New pipes
- Exclusive distributor
- Flexible plastic
- No damage
- Pre-bid jobs
- Entire house
- One day
- Guaranteed
- Specialists
- Multi-unit

- Single-family
- Patch and paint
- Online schedule
- Water pressure
- Lower cost
- Cleaning crew
- Optional upgrades

You've never heard or seen anything about this company, but I'm betting you now have a pretty good idea of what he does and what he might be pitching. Make a note and see how close you are in the chapter coming up.

That's how powerful simplicity can be. Imagine what starts to happen when we refine these bullet points, when they are ordered just right, and when a narrative story connects them together with a powerful hook.

Let me show you exactly how to do that.

CHAPTER 3

WHAC YOUR STORY

My investment-banker uncle, Mark, had talked me into going to Florida for one of his client conferences, where companies tried to raise money from investors. The first presentation I sat in on was by a guy we'll call David, the CEO of a Texas-based oil exploration and production company we'll call Sun Resources. We were in a darkened generic ballroom of a generic chain hotel, with maybe fifty men and women (mostly men) seated at long rows of tables with yellow legal pads poised for notes.

David shyly greeted the crowd and promptly fired up his PowerPoint slides. He spoke for the next twenty minutes, and even though he was speaking English, I struggled to understand what his company did, what he was looking for, or why anyone would invest in his company. He talked about permeability and porosity, dusters and dry gas, geophones and gamma logs.

It wasn't just that his presentation was full of technical jargon—it seemed as if his aim was to dump as much information on his audience as he could, whether or not it mattered to them.

When I caught myself dozing off about ten minutes in, I pinched myself and noticed that the audience was bored to tears. Once he got to his last slide, David asked the audience if they had questions. After a long, awkward silence, David thanked everyone for being there.

Mark tapped me on the shoulder. "See what I mean?"

Mark had lured me down there because he'd seen me help people with their presentations in informal settings, using the same techniques I used to pitch my TV shows, and thought there was an opportunity to help these CEOs improve their presentations. David's presentation was no exception. Mark said he'd nodded off during dozens of presentations.

He then introduced me to David, who was planning to present to potential investors five more times over the next day and a half.

I sat through his presentation again. It was exactly the same, but this time I really focused (stayed awake), and I was able to pick out some interesting and valuable elements about his presentation and company. I made some notes.

RESCUING DAVID'S PRESENTATION

Oh, man. Where to start?

"Can you really still be profitable if oil falls to thirty-two dollars a barrel?" I asked.

The price of oil had just dropped to under forty dollars a barrel for the first time in a very long time, which was causing much concern in the industry. David said yes, and that there were very few companies as well positioned to continue exploration activities with oil below thirty-seven dollars a barrel.

I wrote something on a piece of paper and handed it to him.

"At your next presentation, I'd like you to start with this. Trust me."

He looked at the piece of paper. "So I should put it on slide four, maybe, after I've done the introduction?" He reached for the computer to type it into one of his slides.

"No," I said. "Don't worry about the slides. I mean actually start the presentation with it."

He looked at it again.

"What do you have to lose?"

At the next room of investors, a few hours later, he opened with the lines I'd given him: "Hi, I'm David from Sun Resources. My company has developed several land parcels with full geological and geophysical validation, which translates into far fewer dry holes than the industry norm, giving us a distinct competitive advantage if oil continues to fall as low as thirty-two dollars a barrel."

The room shifted. People perked up. I smiled.

And then he proceeded to go through his PowerPoint presentation again from the beginning, draining the energy out of the room. It was only seventeen minutes later (out of the total twenty-two) that he explained *how* he could keep drilling at thirty-two dollars a barrel.

Facepalm. A few questions, then silence.

Afterward, I asked if I could move around some of his slides. He hesitantly agreed.

I pulled a few of his slides and reordered them and wrote out the beginning again.

"Hi, I'm David from Sun Resources," he began, at the next presentation. "My company has developed parcels that allow us to continue to keep our rigs drilling and remain profitable even if oil continues to fall as far as thirty-two dollars a barrel . . . and here's how we are able to do it."

This was much better. He explained how he was able to keep drilling. This time, there was no doubt the audience was hooked and engaged. But once he got through that, it was back to twenty painful minutes of slides and information for information's sake.

We worked a little more, and by the last presentation, even though it was still almost seventeen minutes, he was getting thirty questions, and they had to force people out of the room for the next presentation.

At the end of the day, David wouldn't let me go. He'd seen the results a few small changes could make, and wanted me to help him overhaul his presentation. I agreed to work with David in Los Angeles, and—thanks to my uncle who kept falling asleep in presentations—I had my first client.

He brought books and PowerPoint slides and binders.

I had five Post-it pads, a notebook, and a black Sharpie.

We started with a key word exercise, and we quickly had dozens and dozens of Post-its covering the entire wall of the conference room.

We worked nearly nonstop for two days. We restructured and rewrote and reordered everything. I knew absolutely nothing about the oil and gas business, but that didn't matter.

rigs	West Texas Intermediate	Brent crude	valley location
easy production	tectonic plates	no finance charges	highway access
OPEC	proven wells	$32 a barrel	well heads
geology	clear leases	$37 a barrel	drill bits
Port of Houston	ample reserves	viscosity	well blockages
tankers			

The information, the value, and the simplicity of his offer were like a universal language. It was absolutely exhilarating.

We rebuilt his PowerPoint, and I arranged it just like I would if I were pitching a TV show. It was now simple, containing only the most important phrases. It was clean and it was clear and it was powerful.

Our company can **keep drilling** profitably even if crude prices drop below **$32 a barrel**.

We have **clear leases** on proven wells with **ample reserves**.

Our geology offers us **easy production** with few **well blockages**.

The **valley location** gives **tankers** quick **access** to major highways to the **Port of Houston**.

Our competitors must stop production below **$37 a barrel**.

His expertise as a former Chevron SVP and his incredibly well-secured financial line made his company a beacon of light in a dismal oil and gas sector. That was his first three minutes.

He then went on to some obligatory financial details, some boilerplate stock performance history, and some projections. When we were done, his entire investor presentation, including the SEC disclaimers and his financial disclosures and prospectus, was just under eight minutes.

He was taking questions and engaging with his audience after eight minutes, instead of his normal twenty-two. People liked what they heard, they understood it, and they saw the value. The results were clear and immediate.

Imagine one of those chainsaw log sculptures that starts out as a giant log and turns into a beautiful carved eagle surrounded by sawdust and wood chunks.

I couldn't tell you which one of us was more ecstatic.

Breaking down David's presentation

I still have the emotional voice mail David left for me after his first pitch three days later.

"Hey, Brant, I just wanted to call and say thank you. The presentations are going amazing, the reaction was exactly what we had hoped for and much more. It looks like I closed at least three new majors, and I was absolutely inundated with questions and follow-up. I don't really know what to say. I've never been comfortable up there doing this but this is just different, I think

I'm actually looking forward to doing more. My wife thinks you put some voodoo spell on me. Anyway, just thought you'd like to know it's going really well, I honestly just can't thank you enough."

To be honest, I was a little perplexed. I wasn't expecting my advice to work as well as it did. This was way before I had developed most of the advanced techniques you're going to learn as we progress through the book. The foundation of what I was teaching went against what most people seemed to believe about sales, marketing, and presenting: That more is always better. That if you were given an hour to persuade an audience to buy or invest in something, you better make sure you fill the whole hour.

I knew after that weekend my life would never be the same. (I wish I'd asked him to pay me in stock because as I write this, it's up fourteen times from that day.) If the simplified pitching techniques I'd developed in the world of television could work in the complicated technical world of oil and gas drilling, could it work with anything?

To answer that question, I set out to work with anyone who wanted help with presenting anything. I met with marketing, investor relations, biotech, and venture capital companies, and teachers, contractors, and doctors. The more I studied and practiced, the more I could see how powerful this technique was.

As I worked with more and more companies, I started to notice a distinct pattern emerging. Each and every time we started down the road to create or restructure a pitch or presentation, we started with the bullet point exercise, and then we'd categorize each of the bullet points. I was asking my clients a series of questions to filter their information. I needed to break down all the elements of their business, product, or service completely so I could reassemble the pieces. The more we stripped it down to the basics, the stronger the foundation to build the presentation.

I found that this process revolved around four specific questions. I could see that these four questions were the pillars of the rationalization story we would be building for their audience. Our bullet points would then be grouped into one of these four categories depending on which question they best answered.

1. **What is it?**
2. **How does it work?**
3. **Are you sure?**
4. **Can you do it?**

It is very simple, but very effective. By using these four questions to filter your information, you can unlock a powerful storytelling technique that will help you lead your audience to the conclusion you want, every time.

I've honed this process to a specific system that I call the **WHAC** method.

BUILDING YOUR STORY
WITH THE WHAC METHOD

You can use WHAC to refine the precise order of your information, and later we'll use it to identify the **level of importance** for each element of your presentation.

As you look at your collection of Post-it notes that represent every word that applies to your company or idea, let's send these notes through these four questions to help categorize your information and give us the foundation to build out your story.

W—What is it?—Does it describe what your offer or ask is? Is it what you do or what service you perform?

H—How does it work?—Does it explain why the elements of your offer are valuable or important? Does it explain how your product works or how you achieve your goal? Is it about the process?

A—Are you sure?—Is it a fact or a figure that backs up some of your information? Does it prove something? Does it validate or establish potential?

C—Can you do it?—Is it something that speaks to the ability to execute or make the offering real for your audience? Is it about you or your ability to execute? Is it how you deliver? Is it about the price?

There is a very specific order to how your audience will most effectively process your information. The WHAC method will allow you to establish and follow that structure.

When building the ideal 3-Minute pitch or presentation, you need to lead your audience through the information and build the story. By simplifying your message in this way, you are really feeding your information in statements and stages that allow your audience to form a core understanding of the value of the proposition. Effectively, you want them to see your proposal the way you see your proposal.

Many people start out wanting to use facts, figures, logic, and reason to explain their value proposition to others. But facts, figures, logic, and reason require **context** to be effective and credible. Context requires a **foundation of understanding**. A foundation of understanding relies on a **solid premise**.

To build an effective story we must begin with a solid premise.

Your audience must first understand the offering, what you do, what it is, why it exists. This must be in the simplest of terms. It must stand alone and allow the audience to fully grasp the **concept**.

Next, they then begin to deal with the **context** of the information as it relates to them and their needs. When they understand what it is and how it works, they try to understand what it can do for them: How is this going to help me?

Once they conceptualize and contextualize your offering, they will look for how to make it real: How do I take **action**? How can I make it happen? How is this going to be executed? Who will deliver it? What does it cost?

This is the format of the 3-Minute pitch:

Conceptualize—What is it and **how** does it work?

Contextualize—Are you sure? Is this true, is it real, is it right?

Actualize—Can you do it? Could this actually happen the way it's being described?

These are three distinct stages to your 3-Minute pitch or proposal. First, you **conceptualize** (explain the offering), then **contextualize** (engage and verify details), and finally you **actualize** (encourage the buy in or opt out).

Look at these stages in a practical application:

0:00–1:30—Conceptualize

1:30–2:30—Contextualize

2:30–3:00—Actualize

Voilà! The 3-Minute Rule.

So as you look at your Post-it notes again through the WHAC filter, you can see how your information will form in groups.

CONCEPTUALIZE

W—What is it?—This is the core of your opportunity. These are the most valuable and compelling elements of the proposal so the audience will understand *exactly* what it is you are offering or asking.

H—How does it work?—This is how it happens, the details or mechanics of how you are able to deliver on that opportunity. You're going to use anything that spells out how what you are saying is possible and why it works. Look for those unique or defining statements that really solidify why you believe in your product, business, or service.

CONTEXTUALIZE

A—Are you sure?—This is where the audience looks to verify your statements and claims. This is where you want to use your facts, figures, logic, and reason. After they understand what it is and how it works, the audience looks for something that backs up your claims. If they can conceptualize and contextualize your offering, they will be looking to validate your claims from a place of enthusiasm.

ACTUALIZE

C—Can you do it?—This is about the ability to actually execute or bring your offering to fruition. It could be your background, experience, or unique circumstances that allows you to deliver. This says you can actually make it real.

The idea is to get all your bullet points into one of these categories. Later you'll see how this early exercise will be the foundation for your entire presentation.

Here is a list of questions I often ask to help ramp up the process. You may find that these questions cause you to grab your Sharpie and add a few more bullet points.

W—WHAT IS IT?

- What makes you unique?
- What can you do that others can't?
- What is the biggest need this fills?
- Are there big monetary advantages to your methods?
- What problem does this solve?
- Who is helped the most by this?
- Why does this have to happen now?
- What will be different after buying in?
- What hole in the market does this fill?
- What could this be worth in success?
- Why is it low risk?
- What makes your competition inferior?
- Why can't someone copy you?
- How easy is this to implement?

H—HOW DOES IT WORK?

- What allows you to make your offering work?
- How can you deliver on your promise?
- How long will what you propose take?
- Is this a gradual or immediate change?
- How many people have this problem?
- Why haven't others used this method?
- Who is actually performing the service?
- Is there a process that must be precisely followed?
- Has this been done successfully in the past?
- Are you taking any shortcuts?
- How is it safe?
- What are the things that only you know how to do?

- Why are there no other ways to do this?
- Why would you choose this method over others?
- How much money will someone save?
- Why is your way the only way?

A—ARE YOU SURE?

- What have you said that someone might not believe?
- Has a third party verified your claims?
- How can this result be replicated?
- How do you know there is a need for this?
- What in your history confirms this?
- Who are you using to deliver this?
- What do your reviews say?
- How valuable is this market?
- How have people succeeded in this before?
- What makes you so sure you're right?
- How did you know you were onto something?
- Why is this not "too good to be true"?
- Has anyone lost money like this?
- Has any of this been announced in public?
- Do you have unexpected supporters?
- Why can't your competition do this better?

C—CAN YOU DO IT?

- What have you done that's similar?
- Why don't the regulations apply?
- Why isn't this restricted?
- Is there anything in your past that would ruin this?

- How have others failed trying something like this?
- How have you trained for this?
- Are there other steps to take before you can deliver?
- Is there any fine print?
- Are there any other third parties involved?
- What successes led you to making this work?
- Do you have this in your possession now?
- What do you do if someone changes his or her mind?
- Do you have the connections that are necessary?
- Is there anyone better suited to deliver?
- What are the repercussions of underperformance?
- Who does someone contact if there is a problem?
- How have you dealt with problems in the past?

Once you've gone through your bullet points and categorized them, place them in columns or groups under each of the four WHAC categories. I want you to separate them out clearly because these are the four pillars that will make up your story and your three minutes.

In the next chapter we're going to expand on these Post-it notes and create statements of value. Then we'll take a look at how we do a "string out" (what we in the entertainment business call our collection of scenes laid out in the basic order) and add some key story elements to build your pitch into a cohesive narrative.

What you may not have noticed is that the WHAC process forced you to explain your bullet points as you categorized

them. You may have even realized you were using a rationalizing story to justify each one. WHAC forced you to simplify
your information, and you may not have ever heard yourself
doing it. That's OK because we're going to do it for real in the
next chapter.

CHAPTER 4

THE STATEMENTS OF VALUE

arly on in my speaking career, I was invited to a conference called NobleCon to conduct a seminar for CEOs from small-capitalization public companies on pitching and presenting. After my seminar, Uncle Mark, the conference organizer, was introducing me to various attendees. While Mark was making introductions, one man nearby kept smacking the table where he was working, and audibly cursing to himself while he stared at his laptop.

"Damn it!" the guy at the table blurted out again. Every few minutes he'd pound on his keyboard and huff and puff something else. Eventually, Mark went over to talk to him.

"Brant, I want you to meet Peter from GTK Therapeutics," Mark said as he brought me over to the man who seemed to be in some kind of distress. Peter was the CEO of a public biotech company. We exchanged pleasantries and then Mark laughed and asked, "Peter, did you enjoy Brant's seminar?"

Peter replied, half annoyed, "I thought it was amazing. But

now I have to redo my entire presentation. Everything you said *not* to do, I've been doing."

"Oh no!" I replied. I quickly looked at his screen, and he was feverishly deleting text from his PowerPoint slides. "See what I mean?" he asked as he scrolled through slide after slide packed with text and graphs and bullet points.

"I'm guessing these are your handouts turned into a Power-Point?" I asked. He just grinned and started deleting and re-typing.

"How many slides do you have?" I asked.

"Thirty-nine."

I resisted the urge to face-palm.

"When are you presenting?"

"In less than an hour. I'm so screwed."

Oh dear.

I scanned through a few more slides.

He is totally screwed, I thought to myself.

His problem wasn't only his PowerPoint slides. Those were just the symptom of a much bigger problem (although I'll address how to use slides effectively in chapter 13).

FIXING PETER'S PITCH

I asked him, "Do you have any business cards?"

"Sure," he said, and handed me one of his cards. I remember the look of disappointment on his face as he thought that I was just going to take his card and call him sometime.

"No," I said. "Do you have a bunch of business cards?"

He fumbled in his laptop bag and came out with a stack. I

took about a dozen and flipped them upside down and laid them on the table. I grabbed my pen.

"OK. Let's start. Give me the single words or phrases that describe what your company does."

He spat out a pile of words and I wrote them down. He introduced me to his wife, Nancy, and she blurted out more items. For example:

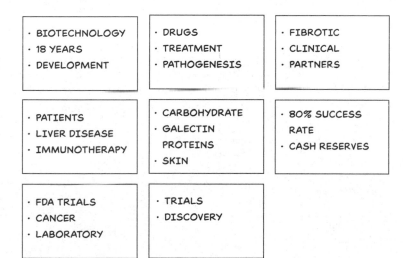

· BIOTECHNOLOGY · 18 YEARS · DEVELOPMENT	· DRUGS · TREATMENT · PATHOGENESIS	· FIBROTIC · CLINICAL · PARTNERS

· PATIENTS
· LIVER DISEASE
· IMMUNOTHERAPY
	· CARBOHYDRATE
	· GALECTIN
	  PROTEINS
	· SKIN
		· 80% SUCCESS
		  RATE
		· CASH RESERVES

· FDA TRIALS · CANCER · LABORATORY	· TRIALS · DISCOVERY	

Peter just stared at me and said what everyone I've ever worked with says the first time we meet: "My company is complicated and it takes time to explain, and there's more to what we do than can be explained in three minutes. We have too much going on."

When I hear this, I usually respond by saying, "No, it isn't complicated. The information is very simple. You are making it complicated."

But this time I was looking at these business cards with words on them that I didn't even know existed, thinking to myself, "Damn, this might actually be complicated."

But I kept going.

"OK," I said. "Now give me words and phrases that describe **what** you **do well**. What makes you more valuable or more interesting than your competitors?"

In a few minutes Peter and Nancy came up with the following:

· LEADERSHIP · MODERN · PARTNERS	· SUCCESS · QUALITY OF LIFE · TIME FRAME	· RESOURCES · OPPORTUNITIES · BACKGROUND
· LEADING SCIENTIST · INDICATIONS	· KEY MEDIATORS · DEMAND · RAPID GROWTH	

He quickly explained each card as I asked him the four WHAC questions. He had to explain most of his bullet points so a nonscientist like me could understand why he wrote them down and why they were relevant.

I had four groups of business cards, and I had heard one sentence about each of them. Now I could see what his company did and what it did well. The value started to appear.

By this point, we had less than thirty minutes left. We needed to move fast.

As quickly as we could, we rewrote and reorganized his PowerPoint slides. Most of our changes involved deleting long, detailed paragraphs and sentences and replacing them with the bullet points or simple phrases he was using to explain things to me.

For instance, one of his slides had over one hundred words on it.

Here's what it became:

- 18 years in development
- Immunotherapy
- Galectin protein inhibitors
- Clinical trials
- 80% success rate
- FDA approval pending

Six bullet points, sixteen words.

We did this to as many slides as we could get through.

We talked it back and forth. We did a test run. It sounded like a huge improvement.

With two minutes to spare, Peter loaded up his new slides and prepared to take the stage.

I sprinted to my seat and looked on with anticipation. I love when my theories get a live test.

It was a total disaster.

I mean a fiery wreck of a burning disaster. Peter stammered through every phrase. He had no idea what slide came next. He was sweating visibly. He was so wildly uncomfortable up there that it made me uncomfortable watching him.

After about five minutes, he stopped and started again, literally reading the phrases off the screen and then explaining them. I felt so bad I wanted to go up and hug him.

If you've ever had a golf lesson, you know the feeling. Your swing works great when the instructor is in front of you explaining it, but the second you get out on the course, there are so many new things running through your head that you can't hit the ball straight to save your life.

This is what I had done to Peter. I had filled his head with so many simplified ideas that he was completely twisted in knots. All of it was there, just the simple elements of his proposal and the basic thoughts about what he did so well. But he just couldn't string any of it together.

When he finally got through his last slide and asked for questions, I was sure the first question (if there were any) would be "How can one person sweat so much and still be standing?"

To my surprise, the room lit up with questions. Every person in the audience had something to add or ask. Once this process started, Peter was in his element. The investors were asking about specific details from the proposal. They were asking engagement questions. They were asking from a place of interest.

Peter was not happy with himself. He was so consumed by his own embarrassment that he couldn't see how effective his presentation actually was. I asked him if he'd ever had that response from an audience after a presentation, and he said not even close. He was so shaken by his personal performance that he didn't realize how well his information had performed on its own, in spite of him.

This was quite revealing.

STORY TRUMPS STYLE

Most of the advice you'll find out there on making an effective pitch focuses on how to present, how to speak in public, how to overcome your nerves. The truth is that none of those things matter very much. Whether your delivery is confident or nervous, whether or not you use your clients' names over and over, whether your tie is blue or red, all the audience really wants is the information. Story trumps style.

Let me just say that again: **Story trumps style. Always.**

That's why the 3-Minute Rule and the WHAC method are so effective. People want to know what it is you are offering, how it works, why it's good, and how they get it. If you get that out quickly and concisely, you'll have an engaged audience looking for more.

Simplicity is powerful. I often joke, "Simple is the new sexy."

Nobody wants to be entertained by what I call "linguistic dancing." Everybody is too busy. They want the most relevant information quickly and concisely.

The most important step is to strip everything you think you need to say down to its simplest, most direct form. The process of conveying everything of value about your offering clearly, concisely, and accurately in three minutes or less begins with a fundamental question:

How can you compress everything you *think you need* to say into *only what needs* to be said?

You are going to be saying less . . . and getting more. You can do this with every pitch or presentation at any time, for anyone and anything.

I urge you to abandon all preconceptions about language, tactics, phrasing, or technique, and focus only on the value of the information and the process of translating that information in a way the audience will understand.

One of my favorite moments working with new clients is when we have that Post-it-covered wall filled with bullet points and we take a big step back and look at everything. I've never had a client look at it without a huge smile. There is something so satisfying about how the simplicity and clarity stares back at you.

If you've got your collection of bullet points from chapters 2 and 3 in front of you on the wall, you're probably feeling the same way.

One of the reasons it looks so good and so clear is that the information represented by these bullet points is perfectly explained in your mind. The process we just went through to get this information down to only words and bullet points forced you to rationalize each thought in the simplest terms.

Now we're going to reverse the process and expand those bullet points back into those simple full thoughts and sentences.

Look at all of your points again and say out loud the details surrounding them. For each one, explain why you wrote that word or phrase down, and why you put it in the WHAC category you did. I bet they sound simple, clean, and clear.

Break these out just as simply as you did when you were explaining them to yourself during the WHAC section. What is the simplest way to say it?

These simplified statements are what I call **statements of value**.

So if your bullet point was:

Personal trainer, *it becomes* I'm a certified personal trainer.

Former athlete, *it becomes* I played semiprofessional baseball.

Low repetition, *it becomes* Low repetition increases intensity.

Rest period, *it becomes* A short rest period increases heart rate.

Celebrity clients, *it becomes* I train actors for athletic roles.

Does this look too simple? Good.

Are you thinking of skipping ahead because it's too basic? Don't. This is just like anything else in life; if you break it down to its simplest form and build the proper foundation, it will allow you to create the strongest possible structure. Pitching an idea, raising money, convincing parents at the PTA meeting, asking for a promotion, marketing your company, and getting board approval are all based on making the foundation of value perfectly clear. So, trust me, write out the simple phrases.

As you go through this process, you'll hear in your mind a story developing. It's important to *stay brief!* You have been living with this information, and you'll find yourself slipping back into phrases and jargon you're used to using. The exercise here is not to fall back on all of your previous sayings and verbiage. You need to force yourself to think simple here. Right now, you just want to build the foundation. All of the bells and whistles are coming up. We'll get to those soon.

Are you done writing your statements of value?

What you might notice is that the thirty bullet points just blossomed into forty or more statements. That's good. Your simplified bullet points often yield other ideas you didn't think of or skipped over. The process of stripping down and building back up opens up some new thoughts, some new statements of value. In those forty or so statements lives the most powerful three-minute version of your pitch.

Now we just need to choose what to say first, what to say later, and tie them all together so the audience understands it like you do.

That's the easy part.

CHAPTER 5

THERE'S MORE TO YOUR STORY

You are probably looking at a collection of more than forty statements of value and thinking, "I thought this was supposed to be a 3-Minute pitch?" I get that a lot. Remember, it's not just about getting it down to three minutes; it's about finding the *best* three minutes. It's most likely in your pitch and presentation you'll get a chance to say and explain every single one of your statements, because your first three minutes are going to have your audience eager and excited to engage further.

But you probably don't have them all yet. In fact, I'm willing to bet there is unmined gold about what you do and what you're offering that isn't sitting in front of you in those forty statements.

I know I told you in the last chapter that we'd be taking your statements and putting them together, but my experience has taught me that our next exercise is going to reveal some of the most valuable elements you haven't thought of yet.

You've been living with your information and understand

it so well that you believe you've got the simplest version; you believe that you've found the core value. You're most likely looking at statements that you've used many times and know extremely well.

I've got a great way of going one step deeper to help you uncover something new. Something waiting to be uncovered.

I DON'T GET IT

I'm not exaggerating. It was seventeen minutes into Michael's presentation when I muted the speakerphone and looked around the room and asked, "Does anyone have a clue what he's talking about?" All six of my executives were staring blankly, saying no, and shaking their heads.

Michael ran an IR (investor relations) company. He helped public companies manage their information and press to communicate to their shareholders and the public.

Michael saw one of my presentations and begged me to help him. I was pretty busy, but I told him I could give him thirty minutes on a conference call to hear his story and his pitch. But no promises.

My TV executive team and I were in a brainstorming meeting in the conference room when my assistant reminded me I had scheduled this call.

"You guys want to hear what a pitch outside TV sounds like?"

We gathered around the speakerphone.

Michael started his slide show on our remote viewer, and off he went.

Seventeen long minutes crept by.

I finally stopped Michael midsentence. "Michael, hold on. Before you go any further, I have to tell you, I don't get it."

"I'm sorry, what don't you get?"

"Basically all of it. I don't really get what you do, not really."

Silence.

"I tell you what, you start again, and I'll chime in when something doesn't make sense."

I told the team to raise their hands when something didn't make sense or they didn't get it

Michael started again.

Four sentences in, one of my executives raised her hand.

"I don't get it," she blurted out.

"Oh, OK, well, that means . . ." And he'd explain a little more.

"Continue."

Two sentences later: "I don't get it." And he'd explain further.

I quickly realized that his explanations were far more interesting and clearer than his pitch lines or slides.

I muted the phone and asked a team member to stand at the whiteboard and write statements of value and bullet points just like we were tackling a show.

After every sentence and slide, I'd say, "I don't get it," and Michael would give a coherent explanation. I just kept saying, "I don't get it."

It may seem absurd that I stopped him every time he spoke. "No, I really don't get it. Explain that." But in the process, we managed to uncover all of the elements that made his business work.

By telling him I didn't understand, he was forced to explain each element, and during that process he had to go deeper into the explanation. It was like each question caused him to keep descending through the layers of simplicity to the absolute rock-bottom core of his information.

For example, he would say, "We employ a stable of free-lance journalists to process the release schedule and maximize reach."

"I don't get it."

"Most IR firms simply send out press releases on a fixed schedule and hope they get picked up."

"I don't get it."

"A public company will have an aggressive release schedule of information, like three times a week. Most of these press releases just get sent out and you hope someone writes an article about it."

"I don't get it."

"The press releases are usually very bland because they are very factual and there are strict regulations on what they can say or promote."

"I still don't get it."

"If you have a real journalist write a story about your company that's factual and sounds interesting, that story is far more likely to be picked up and published."

"I don't get it. How do you do that?"

"I employ hundreds of freelance journalists who write the pieces based on our clients' press releases."

"So you have articles. What does that do? I don't get it."

"Those articles go through our network of news sources. We own news outlets and websites. And we have output deals with every major news outlet in the world."

"I don't get it. Why is that different than anyone else?"

"It means that every time our clients release information about their company, it's going to get written about and it is going to get published."

"I don't get it, is that important?"

"Today, everything an investor uses to assess your stock is initially taken from the research and stories they find about you online. It's all about what people are saying. It's about perception."

"I don't get it. Isn't that what every IR company does?"

"No IR firm can do that! That's why I say we are media and information specialists."

"I think I get it now."

By the time the conversation was wrapped up, I could tell Michael was exhausted. I think he knew I was grilling him out of exercise and not ignorance (I hope), but I was looking at a whiteboard filled with statements of value that were clear. I could see what he did, how he did it, why it worked, and why it was valuable.

"What do you think?" he said.

"I got it. Get on a plane and get out here, I'll help you build a new presentation. You've got good stuff here."

Michael came out the next week and it barely took an afternoon to structure his new presentation.

Michael made pitches to public companies over the phone with remote slides, asking them to hire him on a monthly retainer. These public companies all had other IR firms handling their communications, so Michael was asking them to make a switch.

Michael called two weeks later.

"Before, I was doing ten pitches a month, and I closed one new client every three months. That was enough to keep the lights on. But in the last two weeks, I made five pitches and I closed three of the five!"

Michael was ecstatic. Finally, people could see what his business did and that it was different. That information was standing on its own, a beam of light amid the sameness.

My takeaway was that now that Michael had signed three new clients, each for $25,000 a month, I should have charged him more!

The real lesson, of course, is when you force yourself to explain what you do and why it's valuable, down to the very core, you will reveal things you were probably missing.

At TV development meetings, I started hitting my executives with simple, probing, basic "I don't get it" questions. This was helping us put the information in order, and it was forcing us to come up with more simple and clean statements.

"We're going to find the country's most crooked contractors and expose them."

"Why would we want to do that?"

"Because everyone has had a crappy experience with a crooked contractor."

"So, what does that mean?"

"That means if we can catch them and get justice, people will love that."

"I don't get it. How are you going to do that?"

"We'll set up a sting, like *To Catch a Predator*."

Or,

"Chefs who are overweight, trying to get thin."

"Why is that different?"

"Chefs eat such decadent food as part of their lives, they get fat."

"How is that different?"

"It's a cooking contest, but also a weight loss contest."

"I don't get it. How are those things even connected?"

"They have to eat their own food while they lose weight."

"What would that do?"

"It forces them to learn to cook healthier, so they can lose weight."

"How does that work?"

"They have to cook great food to win the cooking contest, but it has to be healthy enough to still lose weight."

The first of those shows, *Catch a Contractor*, became a huge hit; the other is about to go out to the networks, so it may be on TV as you read this. Fingers crossed.

NO SUCH THING AS A STUPID QUESTION

Blasting yourself with simple "I don't get it" questions will exhaust your knowledge of your proposal. If you do it right, and if you do it long enough, you will uncover every layer and every facet of your pitch.

When I take on a new private client, I spend two or more hours asking stupid questions about every statement about their company. It's exhausting, but it strips everything else away. When you keep asking, "I don't get it, why is that important?" you will find something.

A pharmaceutical company CEO and I got into it in an almost combative fashion. I suspect that as the CEO of a company worth billions, he wasn't forced to answer questions like that over and over.

Cross-examine yourself. Before you commit to any piece of your pitch, before you decide which statements are important and which aren't, you need to put yourself through a serious interrogation.

You won't like it. The first ten questions are easy. You already have those down. It's the next ten that hurt, because you're going to come across some that you can't really answer well (for now).

Say you run a hardware store in Akron, Ohio. If you ask, "Why would someone buy their tools from me and not online or from Home Depot?" and your answer is "Because I'm local," then ask, "Why does that matter?" If your answer is "Because it keeps the money in the community," ask, "Why would anyone care?" Because . . .

If your questioning leads you down a dead end and your answers start to sound less than authentic, go back up the chain and change an answer.

The answer to *"Why would someone buy from me and not online?"* might turn into "Because people want to put their hands on it first."

"But why would that make any difference?"

"Because the price is close enough."

"Why does that matter?"

"Because they'd rather have it immediately than pay for shipping and wait for a delivery if they buy online."

Keep asking questions and keep pushing yourself. The detective work here is important.

Isn't this fun? You started with thirty bullet points. You expanded to forty statements of value, and now you interrogated and questioned yourself into even more. You may be looking at sixty or more statements.

I've never had a client not come up with some more gold when they mined through this interrogation. There is always something of value that pops up.

The more gold there is sitting in front of you, the more powerful your three minutes can be. Now, out of everything you have in front of you (for real this time), I'm going to show you how to filter this down to the actual twenty-five statements that are going to make up your three-minute pitch. This filter will help you decide if something is informing your audience or trying to engage with them. Very important rule: You can't engage with your audience until you've informed them. They must conceptualize before they contextualize; they must contextualize before they actualize.

Now we start having some fun.

WRITING YOUR LOGLINE

After asking your "I don't get it" questions and seeing the simplified answers in front of you, you may be able to put the most valuable element of your offering into a single sentence or phrase. In media and entertainment, this is called the **logline.**

If you take *The Biggest Loser*, the most successful show my company has produced, it was sold to the network president at a Super Bowl party starting with just this logline: "Overweight contestants compete to lose the most weight; the winner is the biggest loser."

This would fit easily into Twitter's old 140-character limit. Could you make a Twitter version of your idea? Try to refine it to a crisp 140 characters (not the flabby 280 characters we're now allowed).

This is where you start to see your information in terms of **must say** instead of **want to say**.

Can you get a logline as concise and information packed as the one for *The Biggest Loser*?

Go to my website, 3minuterule.com, and fill in your Post-it note words in the box provided. I'll send you my logline and you can compare it to yours.

Don't worry if you can't get it just right. I've had clients work for days perfecting their logline. It will continue to evolve as we go through the next chapters.

CHAPTER 6

INFORMATION AND ENGAGEMENT

"Confused people don't buy anything" is a well-known concept from Robert B. Cialdini's 1994 book *Influence: The Psychology of Persuasion*. When you simplify the process for people, those who might have been confused are not confused any longer, and those who instantly understood it feel confirmed in their assumptions.

Without question the number one mistake I see is combining **information** with **engagement**. It is a very easy mistake to make, and it makes pitching and presenting so much harder and less effective than it should be.

Your goal in your 3-Minute pitch is to *inform*, then *engage*.

Think of it like a jigsaw puzzle. You have all the pieces, now let's fit them together to make a perfect picture.

Let's go with the puzzle metaphor for a moment:

If you've ever worked on a jigsaw puzzle, the first thing you do is dump all the pieces on the table. You empty the box and make sure all the pieces are on your table. You've probably guessed by now that those pieces represent your statements of value. With a jigsaw puzzle, the next step (unless you are one of those strange people who do things differently) is to separate the pieces and find all the corner and the edge pieces. Once you get those pieces separated, you build the framework of the puzzle. Once that is done, you fill in all the middle pieces, the heart of the puzzle. And voilà, the picture is complete.

That's exactly what we are going to do. We're going to take your statements and separate them into edge pieces and middle pieces. These are what I call the engagement and information buckets.

Do you remember the bullet-point list from my client that I gave you at the end of chapter 2, asking if you could figure out what he did? Here is his story; see how close you were just from the bullet points.

REPAIRING A PLUMBER'S PITCH

Jeff was the father of one of my youngest son's schoolmates. We saw each other maybe three times a year at school functions. When I booked a five-day heli-skiing adventure and one of my buddies canceled at the last minute, my wife said, "I think Kinder's husband, Jeff, skis." Two weeks later, there we were, boarding a bus for a three-hour ride deep into the British Columbia wilderness together.

Jeff and I sat next to each other on the bus, and once the wheels started rolling, we got talking.

I knew Jeff did something related to plumbing, but I wasn't sure what. So I asked him what he did.

"Well, I guess you'd say I run a plumbing company, but not really plumbing, more of a service company around plumbing but in re-piping homes," he said.

"I don't get it. What do you mean?"

Jeff began talking about copper pipes, and then PEX (a kind of plastic) pipes, and then plumbing contractors and his call center and how his sales guys bid the house and then he contracts out to plumbing contractors, but those contractors had to be certified to re-pipe his way . . . and the wheels of the bus go 'round and 'round . . .

It was a long bus ride, and it seemed as if Jeff's answer to my simple question about his job would go on until we reached our destination.

Jeff was extremely successful at his re-piping business. Big-time successful. Yet all he kept harping on were the "choke points" that were slowing down his incredible process.

There was a frustration in Jeff's voice that I had heard so many times before. He knew his business and knew exactly why it was so valuable. I could see the exasperation written on his face as he struggled to explain what his business was really all about. That's a very common feeling. His core value and product were clear to him, but it always seemed like people weren't "getting it."

There were so many elements to what his business consisted of that Jeff couldn't seem to keep them straight or get them out fast enough. He was constantly correcting or explaining different elements with "but we also," "oh, but we have a way of fixing," "and we can do that too," and "nobody else does this but us."

He had so much to say that was important that he couldn't decide what to say when and in what order. He was a classic mix of too much information and no semblance of how to organize it. His explanation was a mess.

But it wasn't all bad. Several times during the ride, I said, "Wow, that is a great business model," but Jeff's explanation of it was so confusing and detailed that I could easily see why he was having trouble getting everyone on the same page. I can only assume most of his clients weren't trapped on a three-hour bus ride with him.

At one point Jeff said to me, "My wife says you help people pitch their ideas. Do you think I need some work on mine?"

I didn't know Jeff well enough at the time to know if he was being serious or sarcastic. More important, I didn't know him well enough to know if he could handle the truth.

"You have a lot going on, and some amazing stuff. Let me sleep on it and I'll come up with some thoughts."

I spent that night hunched over my laptop going through his website and marketing materials. His short commercials were devoid of valuable information, and his website was packed with overwhelming details. The true value of what his company did was completely lost.

I quickly went through the exercise of putting the key information into twenty or so bullet points. I categorized them with WHAC. They looked good and looked clear. I then expanded each point with the thought behind it:

- Plumbing company *becomes* We are a nationwide plumbing company.
- Re-piping *becomes* We specialize in re-piping homes.
- Water problems *becomes* Re-piping solves most water problems.
- Repair *becomes* We repair and patch the holes for the pipes.
- No major renovation *becomes* We take what has always been a major renovation and make it a minor one.

And so on.

I had about thirty sentences jotted across six pages. Once I could see all the statements of value, I could see his story coming to life.

The next morning, before we hit the slopes, I told Jeff, "I have something for you that is going to blow your mind," and with that we went off to the powder.

Jeff's situation is probably the most common I find: smart, interesting, valuable businesses that are struggling to get the message out in a way people will understand.

You're likely experiencing something similar. You know your value and the most important and unique elements of your business, but you struggle to explain it and don't know in what order to put the information and how to get everyone to understand it.

After dinner that night, I said to Jeff, "I spent a lot of time going through what your company does and why it's great. I want to show you what I've come up with."

There were several other groups of skiers on this five-day trip, so I called one of the guys from another group over.

I told Jeff to explain what his company does and why it's so good.

The guy came over and Jeff started by talking about his re-piping expertise, then rattled off a series of facts and statements. He wasn't being long-winded or overly complicated, but there was just no pattern or flow. Nothing that tied it together and told a story.

Our new friend at the table was polite and feigned interest. He shared some more pleasantries, and then the conversation drifted away to something completely different.

"Watch this," I told Jeff.

I called over one of the other skiers we met that day.

"Kelly," I said, "I just found out what Jeff does for a living and I found it fascinating. I wanted to see what you thought. Jeff's company re-pipes homes. They will re-pipe your entire house, every fixture. You wanna know the twist? When they re-pipe your house, they actually leave the old pipes right where they are."

"Oh, really? How do they do that?" Kelly leaned in.

"They have these new flexible plastic pipes that they feed through and around the walls and connect them at all the faucets. Just like that, new pipes for your whole house."

"Oh, that's really smart, I never thought of that."

"Wanna know the best part?" I continued. "They thread these plastic pipes through tiny holes in your wall and the ceiling. They don't have to rip apart anything."

"What?" said Kelly. "You're kidding. They don't rip off your drywall to get behind the walls and stuff?"

"Nope. In fact, they re-pipe your entire home in just one day, patch all the little holes so there's no mess, no damage. You wouldn't even know they were there. They take what has always been a major renovation and turn it into a minor renovation. You don't even have to leave the house while they do it. Jeff tells me he did an entire hotel while it was still open. They checked into a different suite every day and the guests had no idea. They even wore normal street clothes in the lobby so they wouldn't look like construction workers."

"That's incredible," said Kelly. "How do you connect the new plastic to the old fixtures?"

"Yes, Jeff, how do you do that?" I grinned.

Jeff proceeded to answer this question, which sparked more questions, and more interest. There was some animation at our table now. Soon, another group of skiers came by to check out the conversation.

Kelly said to the new audience, "So Jeff runs a plumbing company that can re-pipe your entire house in one day by feeding these flexible pipes through tiny holes in your walls. They leave the old pipes in place and only run the new ones."

"That's brilliant!" exclaimed the others. "Are the plastic pipes as strong as the copper?"

Jeff then answered his question, and they were off to the races. For the next thirty minutes, Jeff answered questions and talked about his company and how it worked. At one point there must have been fifteen people gathered around.

After everything died down, Jeff was blown away. "How on earth did you do that so fast?"

I told him that most if not all of his problems were the

result of putting the elements of his pitch in the wrong order. He just needed a road map for the audience.

I explained how an audience conceptualizes, contextualizes, and actualizes his information and that it's important to feed an audience the information in that basic order.

The key was identifying the statements about Jeff's business that would inform the audience and the ones that would engage the audience.

Once I was able to inform his audience of the basic concept, get them interested in and understanding how it worked, all the other details about what his company did and how it all worked became engagement points.

There were thirty-two other skiers staying at this lodge for the five-day trip, and by the end of it, every one of them had heard Jeff's pitch and he could see how quickly they understood his information. There were at least a dozen other business owners and entrepreneurs there who watched us unpack and repack his information. By the time the week was done, I had helped a stationery company, a shipping logistics company, a custom home builder, a clinical therapist, a helicopter ski lodge owner, a property manager, and a Realtor. I loved every minute of it. Cracking the value and unique elements of a Dutch financial planner while naked in the sauna was an experience I won't soon forget.

This was a great exercise for me because I noticed that during the entire process I was asking Jeff and the others the same questions as I was of the $2 billion public company clients. What do you do differently, what's unique, what is most valuable? The statements were always different, but the pattern and flow of the information was always the same. WHAC would categorize the information, we'd break out all the statements and filter them through the information or engagement buckets, and the story would start to emerge.

BEFORE AND AFTER

The prolific Academy Award—winning writer Aaron Sorkin once said to me, "The worst mistake you can make is telling the audience something they should already know."

After you've WHAC'd your bullet points, categorized and expanded them, we want to build your story and your 3-Minute pitch by deciding what gets said first, second, and not at all. To do this, we'll play the before-and-after game.

When I work with clients, I usually print or write out on index cards each of their statements of value. Then I'll have the client play this game. I shuffle the cards and arrange them randomly on the table. Starting with any random statement, I ask:

"What information would someone need to know right before this, and what information would they want to know right after this?"

This becomes a quick back-and-forth as it gets the client talking out loud about their proposal. They go through their information and quickly see some obvious befores and afters. These statements become married to each other. Kind of like slotting in two puzzle pieces.

Go through your statements and look for obvious befores and afters. Connect the statements together that are obvious. You should be able to see some statements that move to the front of the line, and, more important, you should see some that keep getting bumped further and further down the line.

Besides those easy ones like "I'm a personal trainer" or "We invest in pharmaceutical companies"—which are the basic "What do you do?"—look carefully at those detailed ones that are deep in your information.

For example, when Jeff says, "You can stay in your house while the work is being done," it's a great statement of value, but you can see that lots of other information needs to be said first to get to this. The question is "Why can you stay in your home?" The answer is "Because they make no construction mess," which leads to another why: "Why no mess?" "Because they only cut small holes." You can see how this framework starts to form.

Go through your statements one by one, and start connecting the ones that fit naturally. To figure out what comes next, ask, "How can I do that?" or "Why Is that important?" or "How does that work?" Also ask, "And then what happens?" and find statements that will come next. Start arranging them like a puzzle in linear order. You will see them connect. Some statements will be on an island and some will be a toss-up of what comes first or next. All of that is OK. Shortly you're going to see how to connect all these together and fill in all the gaps.

The important thing is to order as many of your statements as you can.

What you will notice is that some of your statements need a lot of "before" to be relevant. This is a clear indication that this is an "engagement statement."

You know you have your information and engagement statements mixed up if your audience keeps interrupting to ask questions midstream, if they jump ahead and conclude something too soon, or if they ask you to repeat points you covered before because they didn't understand it as you were saying it.

Questions from the audience are usually a good sign, and they indicate the level of interest you're getting, but you don't want the questions to come from a place of confusion or impatience.

Have you ever pitched or presented anything where you had to say, "Yes, I'm getting to that in just a minute"? Or maybe halfway through your pitch you went off on a tangent and you never ended up getting back to the rest of your pitch? About 99.9 percent of the time that's because you were using engagement information too soon in the process.

What's worse is when this mix-up is very subtle. The audience doesn't stop you or ask questions out of order or get confused because they've already dismissed your information. I hear clients say after a presentation, "It felt really good. I thought they were totally following along, but they just didn't seem to get it in the end." Ouch. I know what that feels like. That's a product of mixing engagement ideas in your pitch where information is needed, eroding the overall effect.

Now we have to face some tough decisions about your information. It all can't advance to the 3-Minute final. It's time to make some cuts.

CHAPTER 7

YOUR CORE 3 MINUTES

I t's time to pull some of your value statements out and put them aside. They will not be making the final three minutes. It's not that they aren't valuable or important; they are just statements that can only be at their maximum value after your three minutes. Your first three minutes isn't about everything you have to say; it's about saying only what needs to be said.

Your goal is to get down to the twenty-five statements that are clearly the most informative. In each of the WHAC categories, you have statements that are going to be effective only after your audience clearly understands and has all the necessary context. You have to be prepared to save some of your favorite statements for after your three minutes.

With a little practice and confidence, this will become second nature and glaringly obvious. You will be able to look at a pitch, separate all the elements, and cut to the core instinctively. Maybe I should say a lot of practice, because I still struggle with this sometimes.

There is a reason the "director's cut" on 99.9 percent of all movies is just a longer, less enjoyable version. There is also a reason very few directors get to show that version. It's because directors (me included) get so close to our creations that we lose our objectivity. We become precious about our information. You want to be passionate about your information, but not precious.

A great director knows how to use just enough scenes to connect the story and let the audience fill in the rest.

An amateur director will shoot and edit a scene like this:

Gary on phone gets an angry look on his face

Close-up on phone as he hangs up

Gary storms to kitchen

He snatches car keys from counter

He gets in car

Close-up on sliding keys in ignition

He backs up car

He squeals tires as he drives away

He grips steering wheel tightly as he drives

He pulls into driveway

He slams car door behind him

He storms up front porch

He pounds on door

Angela opens door

Surprised look—"Gary, you shouldn't be here!"

A great director will shoot the same scene, but edit it like this:

Gary on phone gets an angry look on his face

He snatches car keys from counter

Angela opens door

Surprised look—"Gary, you shouldn't be here!"

A great director knows and trusts that the audience will put the pieces together. You don't need to show Gary driving; you just showed him grabbing the car keys. You don't need to show him pounding on the door; Angela just opened it. I always say that your story from *A* to *Z* doesn't need every letter of the alphabet.

It's important to respect your audience and the knowledge they possess. Many of my clients mistakenly think that simplifying their message means spoon-feeding every thought and detail to their audience. "Simplified" does not mean dumbed down, it's actually just the opposite.

I speak a lot about the **sophisticated audience**. I say the two most important questions you need to ask before creating any pitch or presentation are:

1. What knowledge does my audience already possess? (Remember Aaron Sorkin?)
2. How will they rationalize their decision?

Telling your audience things they already know is a very bad habit. It subtly shows a lack of respect for their time and their intellect.

I KNOW IT'S PAINFUL

Our company had been working on a new show called *The Secret Life of Kids* for NBC. They wanted a funny variety-type family show and had gone out to several production companies for proposals. We had already filmed a dozen different scenes for our sizzle presentation, and the editing process was at least two weeks in. We were just at the point where we needed to start building the pitch for the network.

We went to the Post-its:

The show seemed pretty clear, and everyone who saw the Post-its could see where we were going. (You may not know the show or make TV for a living, but I bet you get the idea from these nineteen Post-its.)

While we were going through WHAC and expanding our statements of value, I looked at a rough cut of the sizzle tape. It was twelve minutes long.

My editor and producer said they felt the final piece would run around nine minutes. I happened to be on a high from all my 3-Minute pitches working so well, but I thought this might be different. This wasn't a simple pitch of a TV show, it

was a full presentation of a complete concept that we had spent an incredible amount of time and resources preparing. I felt because we had fourteen different scenes and seven pages of voiceover that this pitch warranted more time. I asked them if they could get it down to six minutes. They looked at me like I was crazy.

Four days later they had it down to 6:21. "This is as much as we could cut, and I think it's missing a lot," said the editor.

I watched it. It was good, but I felt that it was more than we needed.

I copied the words and phrases from the Post-its in the development office and handed them to the editor. "This is all I want to say. No more than five minutes." He was less than enthused.

Three days later, it was 5:12.

"OK," I said, "This still doesn't do what I want. Let's try again. I want this less than three minutes. And I mean less than three minutes. Not one second more than three minutes."

This time I could almost feel a mutiny forming. But I held firm.

This wasn't easy. There were full scenes we had spent days filming that we wouldn't be able to find room for. Imagine how hard it is to cut something when you can see it on a screen. It's literally sitting there filmed and created, and I'm having to throw it away. So I can understand my clients' pain when I tell them to cut out ideas and material they've spent years creating.

While the edit team was struggling with the video, I decided to do the same thing with the printed materials. We had made a twenty-seven-page PowerPoint presentation on how the show worked. I said, "Nope, I want this in no more than seven slides."

Three days later, we sent a 2:58 sizzle tape and seven-slide deck to the network. NBC bought the show.

We filmed scenes at a cost of at least $20,000 that we never showed the network. It doesn't matter how much you like your information or how much you've invested in it; the only thing that matters is what gets the job done.

Now, I can't tell you that they bought it because it was just a three-minute tape and that they wouldn't have bought it if it was nine minutes long. Perhaps the idea was good enough that they might have bought it even with a mediocre pitch.

But here's what I can tell you for sure. From that day on, I never made a sizzle tape longer than three minutes. Not a single one. I'm talking about the next five hundred pitches in my career and not a single one longer than three minutes. Every presentation and slide show we did was never more than ten slides total.

Say less. Get more.

I know it hurts, but you can always cut more.

ONE MORE WHAC

I've been doing this for a very long time and I still catch myself becoming precious with my information. I find that once I get to this stage of creating a pitch or presentation, I have to take a step back and make sure I'm following my own advice.

WHAC'ing the book you're reading

Even when writing this book I had to go to my Post-it notes to get my first draft finalized. I had the book finished, but editing down to what would ultimately be submitted required this very crucial step.

So as your final exercise to help lock in your twenty-five core statements of value, I want you to put them through the WHAC filter one more time.

This time take note of the specific value each section of the WHAC filter has in the overall presentation.

W—What is it?—**50 percent**—Your core concept and being able to make the audience understand the fundamental elements the way you do is *half* the battle.

H—How does it work?—**30 percent**—If they understand how you got to your core concept and how it works, you're now more than three quarters of the way there.

The what and how make up 80 percent of the audience's buy-in decision. If they understand the concept and the value you've laid out, they will be eager to verify and engage. They will be looking for this to work out.

A—Are you sure?—**15 percent**—The facts and figures that back up or verify your offering actually make up only a small portion of that buy-in decision. If you've got your audience there on your what and how, and they are looking to verify from a place of enthusiasm or optimism, it's actually a smaller piece of the puzzle than you would normally assume.

C—Can you do it?—**5 percent**—This is the smallest piece. Depending on the value you've created in the questions above, the answer to this question can be almost inconsequential. For example, with *The Biggest Loser*, the producer with the original idea wasn't equipped to make a show that large or complex. The network was so on board with the concept and potential of the show, they just went about solving the issue by bringing my company on to physically produce it. It wasn't going to derail the process because they were already 95 percent there.

The stronger your information and value, the less important the "Can you do it?" becomes.

So when you cut some of your statements from the final 3-Minute list, look at the number you have in each of the WHAC categories.

Use this as a guide:

W—What is it?—nine statements—1:30

H—How does it work?—seven statements—1:00

A—Are you sure?—six statements—0:20

C—Can you do it?—three statements—0:10

DON'T BE TOO LITERAL

As you look at the WHAC questions, don't take the descriptions too literally. It's the themes and the values that are important, not the literal descriptions.

Your job is to look at these questions and descriptions, understand the level of importance for each, and then match them with what you are proposing. What is the most valuable and compelling element of your pitch? That's your "What is it?" I find that's the one area my clients get hung up on when using WHAC to assemble their presentations: they can be too literal with the questions.

It's worth looking at a few examples to help you feel more comfortable with this.

Remember David and the oil company that could keep drilling even at a low oil price?

Their ability to actually secure, maintain, and drill with various land rights and fluctuating oil prices was valuable and important. They had the ability to keep drilling even if oil prices fell to thirty-two dollars a barrel. At the time, oil prices were at about thirty-nine dollars, and everyone was in a panic because companies across the state were idling their rigs at that price. In this instance, the answer to "What is it?" wasn't that they were a company that drills for oil.

In David's presentation, the core of the "What is it?" was "We're a company that can still pump at thirty-two dollars a barrel." And part of the "How does it work?" was "This parcel of land has deposits 30 percent denser than originally mapped, and the sediment layers require no additional support or relief wells." For an audience that knows about and is interested in investing in oil and gas, this was 80 percent of the buy-in process. The "Can you do it?" was about how they hadn't had any major environmental incidents and that the lease contracts were certified. For his audience, answering the "Can you do it?" question was about saying, "There isn't anything out of the ordinary that will prevent us from doing the job we already do and have been doing for years."

Let's look at another example to really see how the structure of WHAC works and how it's about what is most valuable and not the literal descriptions.

During the 2000s, Mark Burnett was the hottest producer in the reality TV business. He had *Survivor* and *The Apprentice* on the air as the number one and two shows in the ratings. He had become a celebrity simply because of his producing success.

There wasn't a network in existence that wasn't clamoring to take a pitch from Mark Burnett. He had the hot hand, and nobody in the reality TV business had ever seen anything like it.

Mark had a new idea. It was called *Pirate Master*, and it was like *Survivor* on a pirate ship. If you were the last one on the ship, you got to keep the treasure.

Here's how it looked through the WHAC filter:

The most valuable and important element of this show was ***not the show at all***. Mark Burnett was at the top of the food chain. He was the first celebrity reality TV producer. He was doing things with international formats and branded content that nobody else was doing. He also had two smash hits on the air. Everybody wanted his next big project.

So what do you think the most valuable element was about his next idea?

When it came to **W—What is it?** The answer was: "It's Mark Burnett's latest idea and he thinks it's going to be the next global sensation." That was, by far, the most important element. That is, in fact, what it was. The first ninety seconds of the pitch was Mark telling the buyer how much he believed in the project, how he knew how to craft a winning formula, and how this was going to be his biggest show yet. He didn't have to utter one word about what the show was or how it worked.

Can you see it? The most important element of this show was that the number one producer in the world believed this was going to be his next hit. This was the most important thing for the network buyer to conceptualize. Mark Burnett believed in it.

The **H—How does it work?** It wasn't "How does the show work?" It was "How did Mark Burnett get so excited about this idea?" He talked about how it was a *Survivor*-type show that featured contestants playing pirates competing for treasure. Without question the network was at least 80 percent sold.

The **A—Are you sure?** In this case the facts and figures that were validating or confirming the idea had some format elements (sixteen contestants; on a real ship; we eliminate one each week; $1 million prize). You'd think that how the show actually worked would be important, and most times you'd be right, but in this case these were just validation that it had some substance. Fifteen percent at most here.

The **C—Can you do it?** This was really just about Mark saying he would be personally available to oversee the production and that he knew where he wanted to film it.

It sold in the room, and he produced fourteen episodes for CBS. This is an extreme example of how you don't have to take the WHAC questions literally.

Really get creative with your interpretation of these questions. It not only will help you stay focused on your most valuable elements but also will make the order of your information and the flow of your presentation clearer.

But most important, it will help you make your final cuts and leave you with the twenty-five core statements of value that make up your 3-Minute pitch.

In the next chapters we are going to add all of the elements that bring your pitch or presentation to life. But first we'll do another, really fun, test.

THE FIRE ALARM TEST

This is a great exercise I use with clients when we first start to filter their statements of value. Picture yourself in a meeting presenting to an audience. Three minutes into your pitch, just as you are ending, the fire alarm goes off. The room evacuates and everyone is ushered out into the street. (This actually happened to me at MTV once.)

Now ask yourself three questions:

1. Would the audience want to come back in and hear more?
2. If you didn't get to go back in, would they have enough information to make a decision, or is there something you still needed to say?
3. If they were to explain your pitch or proposal to someone else, what would they say?

It's important to be impartial about this. Particularly question number two. I find a lot of people still hold on to something important they are building to. They get this idea that a big reveal or an aha moment way at the end can help. They haven't read the previous chapters.

But you have, and that's why I bring this exercise out early with a new client. I don't want them saving something for later.

Once you're comfortable with your answers and you've adjusted, I want to you to do the exercise again. This time, though, time your presentation and stop after two minutes. The fire alarm goes off. Same scenario. How do you feel about what got cut off?

Which part was it? How do you feel about what the audience didn't hear? Does your message still resonate? Would they want to come back in the building and hear more? Could they explain it to someone else if they got asked, "Hey, what was that pitch about before the fire alarm went off?"

Again, try to be impartial. What you may find is you have used some fun language or phrases that you love but have pushed some relevant information too far down and the early fire alarm killed it.

I still struggle with this. I like clever sayings and details. I like to lead my audience, and sometimes I have to take a step back and really look to see if I'm adding fluff for fluff's sake.

I'm in the middle of a huge game show pitch right now that tests the contestant's ability to instantly recall information. In my proposed pitch I'm dying to talk about the science of how the brain processes memory and what it deems important. And I have a great phrase and line about how "you have no idea how much information you really know." But it's slowing my explanation of how the game functions, and if the fire alarm went off at two minutes, it would not be as strong. So I just reordered the pitch to pack a lot more up front.

Now repeat the exercise at one minute. That's obviously not enough time to pitch your idea. But if you really look at your first minute, could you get someone to come back in and hear more? The answer has to be yes, or you need to adjust.

Take a look at your logline again. Look at that Twitter version. Have you readjusted?

These exercises will help you finalize the order of your information. In an eight-second-attention-span world, capturing and holding your audience's attention for an entire three minutes is a Herculean feat.

Many people mistakenly assume that the 3-Minute pitch is just condensing a long-winded explanation into a brisk three minutes. No, most of what you've been doing here in this book is learning how to make three minutes impactful and interesting enough to get your message across in the most effective way. It's about keeping your audience focused long enough for you to create the desire.

I've heard hundreds of pitches that made three minutes feel like a painful eternity. Timing is a tool. It's no substitute for content.

CHAPTER 8

THE HOOK

A story needs a hook. A song needs a hook. A movie needs a hook. Your 3-Minute pitch needs a hook.

What is a "hook"?

It's the one thing or element about an idea or story that make you go, "Ah, that's cool."

"Cool" is the perfect word for that feeling of acceptance and understanding and approval.

Now, whether that's a funny thing, a price thing, a life-saving thing, or an emotional thing doesn't matter. In context, "it's cool" is what you're looking for.

You have a hook. You have something that someone who knew everything about your company or proposal would met-aphorically say about it, "Ah, that's cool."

I've taught these pitch and presentation techniques to my oldest son, and much to my dismay he uses them against me anytime he wants something. I have a beautiful 1969 GTO Judge convertible, cherry red with a pristine white interior. And when my son comes to me and asks if he can drive it, he knows to lay out his case cleanly and concisely, and he always layers in his hook: "You know I love this car as much as you do and I've never let you down yet." And while I don't directly say it, metaphorically that's the "Ah, that's cool." It's the "He's right." Yes, he describes the date or the event and why it's important for him to take the GTO, but he knows the hook that he loves the car as much as I do and has never let me down before is that thing that grabs me and gets me to say yes.

Now that you have a collection of your core statements and you've got them in a specific order, let me show you how to find and use your hook like a world-class Hollywood screenwriter.

WORKING WITH THE 49ERS

I had always been a San Francisco 49ers fan growing up, so the chance to work with the team and the NFL was a big moment for me.

On one of our first projects together, their president, Paraag Marathe, and I had developed a TV show around NFL team chefs competing against each other in a weekly cooking competition. After developing the show together with the NFL, we pitched it to the networks. It didn't sell, but we formed a lasting friendship.

Paraag's first major task when he became president of the team was to build a new stadium. Imagine a nearly $2 billion project that you have to build in Northern California. How hard could that be?

The team's old stadium, Candlestick Park, was literally

falling apart. There were two choices: either build a new stadium, or move the team. The owners, the York family, had decided they would never move the team, so this was build or die.

The family arranged to borrow the money to build, and in doing so they had to put up the team as collateral. Effectively, they would lose the team if the stadium didn't get built.

Among all the other issues surrounding the construction, which landed on his desk, Paraag also had to find a naming sponsor and a dozen other high-level corporate sponsors to fund the project. Every element required a new pitch, a new presentation, and a new hook.

When you start building a new stadium, you start with nothing besides drawings and mock-up logos. It's all just a theory drawn on pretty paper. Paraag needed to attract huge sponsors to the project and fast. The organization was deep into the construction phase and they still hadn't found their naming rights sponsor. It was the big target, and the tension and pressure were ramping up in every board meeting. This was priority number one.

Time to get to work devising a new pitch.

Sports marketing departments for major corporations hear dozens of sponsor pitches for stadiums and buildings and ad campaigns every year. As you'll see in later chapters, this understanding of "what the audience knows" was a crucial factor in building the proposal for the 49ers' stadium.

The pitches were clean and crisp, and contained only the most relevant and valuable information. The hook for each pitch was different. The pitch to Time Warner or Verizon would have a slightly different hook than one for JetBlue or Honda.

The pitch for Levi Strauss to put its name on the stadium was classic and simple. All the elements and details are clear and clean when put through the WHAC system. Size of stadium, number of seats, media exposure, return on investment, signage. That was the easy part. But all that information needed a hook to bring it to life.

The hook for Levi's was that Levi Strauss was founded in the gold rush. It's a California company. The forty-niner is a miner. It's a California team. Not only that, the Levi's and 49ers' logos had exactly the same shade of red. That meant every piece of merchandise and decorated or painted item in the entire stadium, including the players' uniforms, would contain Levi's red. The brands were meant to be together.

"Ah, that's cool!" We had our hook, and that's why it's called Levi's Stadium today.

But Paraag and I weren't done. As it turns out, building the stadium was just the beginning. Next, Paraag had to fill it. And I'm not talking about football crowds. I was surprised by how much business a stadium has to generate outside of the football team. An NFL team plays at home ten times a year (a couple of games more if they make the playoffs). You can't survive with a stadium sitting empty for the other 355 days a year. The team has to sell high-level executive box seats and corporate suites for as much as $500,000 a year for access to all of the events at the stadium. The stadium needs to book a lot of high-profile events such as major rock concerts.

A big part of Paraag's job was to help secure these high-profile events. I had no idea how important that was until he asked me about my time working with World Wrestling

Entertainment, better known as WWE, and its boss, Vince McMahon.

As it turns out, the annual WrestleMania is one of the biggest sporting events in North America, second only to the Super Bowl. No other concert or event even comes close. What I didn't know was that each year, stadium owners from across the country make the annual pilgrimage to Connecticut to meet with Mr. McMahon and the WWE to pitch (beg, really) for WrestleMania.

"Why?" I asked Paraag

"WrestleMania is the single biggest draw to a stadium and to a community, period. The amount of money and new traffic and demographics it brings are second to none."

This was all news to me. I loved the WWE as a kid, and I had worked with them on a fantastic competition series we did together called *Proving Ground*. I was stunned at the reach and ferocity of their audience. On *Why I'm Not . . .* , my podcast, I once recorded an episode about the WWE and its staying power in the market today, and, to date, it's my highest-rated and most-listened-to episode. But to hear the president of an NFL team agonize over putting together the pitch to get WrestleMania was a little surreal.

Once I understood the stakes, the real concern was "promotion." I'll talk about this in detail later, but there is a fine line between being passionate and being promotional. Passionate is inspiring. Promotional is creepy. I often say, "The more you focus on your desired result rather than your vision for the project, the more likely you will trade passion for promotion." If your audience smells how bad you want it, they will detect desperation, and that erodes everything you've worked for.

You could say Paraag and team were desperate or, to put it more kindly, wildly passionate to the point of absolute need and overwhelming desire. My concern was that that subtle difference would get lost and be mistaken for actual desperation.

Vince McMahon is a legendary businessman, and he feasts on desperation.

Here's how this all went down.

Every year, over the course of a couple of weeks, Vince brings in all of the owners one by one to his offices and lets them pitch their stadium and answer the question "Why should we pick you?" Everybody gets a thirty-minute meeting, and he makes the ultimate decision.

There are only a handful of stadiums in the country large enough to hold WrestleMania, so it's usually the same group of owners parading through.

In 2015, Paraag and Jed (the team owner) and the mayor of Santa Clara flew out to Connecticut to pitch Vince McMahon. It's a prerequisite that you bring the mayor of your city. You need to be able to explain how the city is on board and will provide all the logistic elements to pull off such a massive event. And besides, Vince loves the idea of mayors and stadium owners coming to kiss the ring.

When I heard that all the mayors from all the towns were coming, something dawned on me. Everyone will be saying the exact same thing. Each stadium is going to have the exact same pitch. Why does Vince need you to come to Connecticut? All of the data is available. Seat number, parking structure, flight patterns. All that is basically the same.

There were stories and rumors around about those meetings, and how Vince started the meeting with "So why should I pick you?" as his opening line and then grilled the owners and mayors for thirty minutes straight. I'd heard that sometimes the owners never got a chance to make their pitch because Vince dove into questions and never let up. It makes sense, if you think about it. If you were Vince and WrestleMania was going to be the biggest event on the continent and you were going to make millions and millions regardless of where you held it, wouldn't the only question you ask be "Why should I pick you?"

Paraag would focus on "Why should I pick you?" but he needed a hook. He needed the "that's cool" moment. He couldn't go in there and say, "We have a new stadium, it's really shiny and nice, it seats eighty thousand, and the city will help us throw the event." Jerry Jones would have said the same thing about Dallas five minutes before.

In the WHAC context, I was stuck on "What is it?" The question of "Why should I pick you?" was going to be the "What is it?"

Imagine going through your bullet points, extending them into sentences, before-and-aftering them, filtering and categorizing them through the WHAC system, and finally realizing that the "What is it?" isn't obvious. It's not about the stadium size or how they'll deal with the fans. "What is it?" was something nobody thought of at first.

Paraag was about to pitch his stadium to the biggest event in the world, and his "What is it?" had nothing to do with the physical stadium.

In the lobby of the WWE is an enormous statue of Andre the Giant, a seven-foot behemoth who looms over people waiting for meetings. There is a handprint formed in granite from Andre's hand that invites visitors to try their hand for comparison. It's a humbling experience. A grizzly bear would feel small in that lobby. It's all by design.

Paraag and team were ushered into the main conference room. At the far end of a thirty-foot conference table sat Vince McMahon; on his right side sat his daughter, Stephanie; and on his left, the wrestler known as Triple H (Vince's son-in-law, Paul Levesque).

After introductions and pleasantries, the mayor of Santa Clara gave a brief introduction to the city, said how excited he was, and shared some city details. That served as their opening and reason for being (all details I'll explain more in forthcoming chapters).

Vince got right to it. "Gentlemen, why should we give you WrestleMania?"

Then Paraag began. Here are some of the core statements:

(What is it?) This is the opportunity for WrestleMania and the WWE to be at the center of the digital world. The biggest and most influential companies in social media and technology are in Silicon Valley.

(How does it work?) Levi's Stadium is in the center of Silicon Valley. It's become the iconic building that represents the valley. Facebook, Twitter, Instagram, Salesforce, Cisco, Google, and more have their corporate headquarters surrounding the stadium, and many have corporate boxes.

(Are you sure?) The world is digital; the world is social media. Santa Clara and Silicon Valley are the center of the digital and technological world. It's not just physical location, it's part of the culture.

(Can you do it?) Levi's stadium holds seventy-six thousand for football and will be able to hold almost ninety thousand for WrestleMania. The stadium is brand new and has every possible amenity.

Those were the basic statements in the pitch. But Paraag had also layered in **the hook**. And everything in his pitch played into it.

PARAAG'S HOOK

For Paraag, the hook was clear. Here it is:

With help from those tech icons in their backyard, Levi's Stadium has a unique app that allows anybody in the audience to order food and, more important, merchandise from their seat to be delivered to their seat. No lines, no weaving through the concourse. No other stadium offers that.

Vince McMahon and the WWE will make more money on merchandise at Levi's Stadium than any other stadium in the nation.

The entire pitch took just about three minutes before Paraag turned to Vince for questions.

Let me explain how that hook fits into Paraag's pitch and how it's used in the 3-Minute Rule.

If you look at the hook, it has two parts, **the statement** and **what it means**: (a) it's a system that allows fans to order merchandise at their seat, and (b) the WWE will make more money on merchandise because of it.

The hook needs some context to be effective. As we go through Paraag's pitch, you can clearly see that before you can get into the seat system, you need to establish the "What is it?" and the "How does it work?" to set up the hook.

Here's how it went.

The world is digital; the world is now social media. This is the opportunity for the WWE to be at the center of the digital world.

Santa Clara and Silicon Valley are the center of the digital and technological world. The biggest and most influential companies in the world in social media and technology are here in Silicon Valley.

Our stadium is the most technologically advanced ever built. We worked with the technological titans in our backyard to create an app that allows the audience to order merchandise from their seats. They order during the event, while emotions are running high and the excitement is fresh.

This system has massively increased our in-game merchandise sales, and it will do the same for WrestleMania.

When you understand and hear the app described in context, you figuratively and literally say, "Ah, that's cool."

And that's exactly what Vince McMahon said. Because once the questions started, most of what Vince was asking centered on the technology and the impact of the app and how they could use it to their advantage. Vince actually said at one point, "That's pretty cool."

In 2015, WrestleMania 31 was held at Levi's Stadium.

One of the biggest events in the history of the state of California was pitched and sold in one meeting that lasted less than thirty minutes.

That's how you use a hook inside your story.

FINDING YOUR HOOK

How do you find and use a hook for your story?

First, let's look at your answers for the WHAC method. You should be able to identify one or two of your core statements that excite you the most. If the audience understood your offering perfectly and you asked them, "What's the best part?" their answer is probably your hook.

You can check like this:

Start with a statement of value that you feel could be your hook. In this case we'll take Jeff's plumbing company. His hook is "We take what used to be a major renovation and make it a minor renovation."

So now take that phrase and unpack why it is that important. For Jeff you end up here:

Because a major renovation makes a huge mess

Because a major renovation costs big money

Because during a major renovation you have to move out of your house

Because a major renovation is going to stress you out

Because re-piping an entire house is a huge improvement

Because if you need new pipes you probably haven't done it because of the mess and stress

Because people see a minor renovation as cheap and easy

Because it says my company has some new or unique system

Once you unpack it, you'll see it's that moment when you want to burst out, "Great, right?!"

You don't have to be a genius to understand exactly what Vince McMahon wants most. He wants to make money. But that's not his only motivating factor. For Vince, it can't only be about the money. That can't be your only offering to him. Otherwise WrestleMania would just go to the highest bidder. Same with Jeff. It can't just be the fact that it's a minor renovation. You need all the context.

DON'T OPEN WITH THE HOOK

Finding the hook for most companies is pretty easy. When I ask people for one sentence that nails it—the "Ah, that's cool"—they usually come up with it pretty quickly. But *most* of the time they come out with it too quickly.

Many people, and unfortunately many sales books and coaches, have the misconception that the hook is what you open with.

"Hi, I'm Jeff from Re-Pipe Specialists, and we can take your whole home re-pipe from a major renovation to a minor renovation. Let me show you how."

That sounds good. It might have even sounded right to you before you started reading this book (I'm hoping it's having that kind of impact).

And, yes, it's possible this used to work well in the days when the "elevator pitch" was a thing. The idea being that when you drop that opening on someone in an elevator, they are going to say, "Hmm, interesting, tell me more." You see this idea repeated today by a lot of experts (and nonexperts).

But today, that's not really what most people think when they hear that kind of opening, even if that's what they say out loud to you.

What they're really thinking when they hear that opening is, "I'm not sure I believe you. Prove it." Or, if your statement is even more grandiose, "Bullshit" is the first thought that runs through their head. Then it becomes your job to convince them otherwise.

Does that sound like a winning strategy?

This is called the **state-and-prove** method, and it's been the standard for decades. Unfortunately, it's still taught as Sales and Marketing 101. The idea is that you get someone to desire the outcome first and then use your information to convince them that your statement is true.

The saying I use with everyone is "If you start with a grand conclusion and then try to back it up, your audience will doubt you and look to disprove it."

Think about it.

Why would you want to get your audience thinking, "That's not possible. I don't think so. No, you won't"? Yes, you may win them over eventually, but in that scenario everything you say next has to convincingly validate the claim you just made with the hook. That's just not a good position. You've just created an uphill battle.

All the biotech companies I work with begin their presentation with something like "We are going to revolutionize the health care industry." Besides the fact that that's not a very good hook in the first place, the reaction is usually: "Really? You are? I find that unlikely, but go ahead and tell me more." At that point the best outcome is that someone says at the end of the presentation, "Yeah, it's good, but I don't know about revolutionizing the industry."

Does that sound like a position of strength? When I was running the TV network TLC, producers would come in and open with "I've got a new show that will be your biggest hit!" or "The audience is dying for something like this," or "This is an advertiser's dream."

Is that the way you want to start a pitch or presentation?

State-and-prove is an old and now-inefficient model, particularly in the era of hyperinformation. Technology, marketing, and advertising have advanced radically over the last twenty years. Marketing, fed by billions of dollars a year spent trying to influence you at every turn, has become so sophisticated and effective over the last few decades that there is no part of your life that isn't being influenced by branding. You and I are being targeted, every day, for every part of us. Our age, our gender, our education, our income level, our marital status, our buying habits. It never ends.

To be fair, there is some science that backed this state-and-prove method. It's the study of **approach motivation**, or why people are motivated to make decisions or "buy in." The conventional wisdom was that *desire* creates *focus*, meaning that if you desired something, you focused on it. So our marketing, sales, and advertising world set out to create your desire for the product, which would get you to focus on it, thereby allowing them to explain all the details needed to win you over.

Science says that if you tell me you have my next hit TV show and I'm a network buyer in desperate need of a hit TV show to save my job, I'm certainly going to listen. That may be true, but in today's climate, even while I listen, I'm doubting and judging you.

Yes, if I told you that by reading this book you'd double your sales conversions and triple your income, you'd absolutely desire that outcome. And you might even be willing to focus and listen to what I had to say. But every single fact or statement I said from that moment would be set for or against my promise.

There is a much better way.

The *Journal of Motivation, Emotion, and Personality* released a study that discovered something groundbreaking: approach motivation works in reverse as well. What they discovered was that **Focus can CREATE desire**. Meaning if you can capture and maintain your audience's focus, you can actually create and build their desire for your outcome. You can lead your audience to want and desire your offering, as they hear and understand it.

The science of it may be groundbreaking, but Hollywood has been using this "focus creates desire" method for decades. Leading your audience with storytelling to the conclusion you want (and they want) is the staple of Hollywood screenwriting. You know the good guy is going to win, and you *want* the good guy to win after ninety minutes of leading you. You know how it's going to end, and you *want* it that way. Sure, in a mystery there are big reveals and twists, the "whodunit" factor. But that big reveal is only satisfying if the audience feels they should have seen it coming, based on the previous scenes and setup. This is the basic structure of any good story. You lead your audience.

What you want to do is to start with the facts, plain and simple, and let them build to your grand conclusion. You want the audience, after hearing your what and how, to start to form your hook for themselves. So when you finally say it, in their mind, they will say, "That's right."

I always tell my clients that **the hook is something you almost don't need to say**.

When Vince McMahon heard about the connection to the tech world and the ability to sell merchandise to the audience in their seats, he was already thinking, "I can make more money in merchandise at Levi's Stadium than anywhere else."

But if Paraag had started with "We can make you more money in merchandise than any other stadium in the country," Vince's first thought would have been "Prove it," and he'd be questioning and judging every statement against that.

After Jeff explains that his company only cuts small holes and feeds the flexible pipes through the walls, that there is no mess and you don't have to move out of your house, his customers are thinking before he says it: "This isn't even a major renovation."

The hook almost doesn't need to be said. Your hook should be self-explanatory. That's what you want. That's the power of a great story that leads you through it.

Because we are being marketed to and sold to everywhere we go, we've learned to treat all claims with distrust and skepticism. Every statement and promise and offer are going to be scrutinized, instinctively, by your audience.

Any promises you make that are better than the competition will be perceived as too good to be true. And even if your audience believes your offer has real value, they will start to look for what strings might be attached. It gets worse. If you also use some big adjectives like "revolutionary" or "greatest," they think, "I'm being tricked. This is waste of time."

Your presentation has to go against that grain. You're not going to start with "This is an amazing deal." You are going to set the stage and feed out information so that your audience will naturally conclude, "That is an amazing deal," without your having to say so.

Look at your statements of interest again. Pull out your biggest promises, your summarizing statements, your opinions on how good it is. Take anything that speaks to your hook, and set it aside. Let's focus on the what and how sections of the WHAC filter first. You want your statements to lead up to your hook. You should be able to see the buildup happen right before your eyes.

If you haven't done so already, write all your statements on index cards. The ability to move them around is extremely helpful to the process. You could move these around on a screen, but nothing beats the speed and fluidity of having physical cards you can move by hand.

KATY PERRY IS THE GREATEST EVER

Here's one of my favorite examples to illustrate state-and-prove, which I used in a recent keynote I gave to the National Speakers Association. I was curious to see how a room full of professional speakers would react to my theory of approach motivation.

I put a big picture of Katy Perry up on the screen. I said, "I'd like to introduce you to one of my friends, Katy Perry. I know you know her and her music."

Then I put up my statement:

"Katy Perry is the most successful female performer in history."

The crowd's reaction was a kind of confused silence, until, a few seconds later, I heard a big burst of objection from a corner. "Whhhhaaaaaaatttttttt!"

I smiled and asked the audience, "Does anyone here not *100 percent agree* with this statement?"

Every hand in the room went up.

In one corner, I spotted an elegant older African American woman, Jamilla, who could barely stay seated. Her hand waved back and forth defiantly.

"Anyone actively *disagree* with this statement?"

I could see her twisting in her seat. Everyone put their hands up again.

"OK, wow, does anyone absolutely and wholeheartedly disagree with this statement?" And I walked over to the woman in the corner.

"You look like you don't agree."

"Boy, you must be out of your goddamn mind!" she said, and launched into a very funny rant about her soul sister Tina Turner and my unacceptable, uninformed, and blatantly wrong statement. The audience laughed.

With the show of hands and Jamilla's tirade, I'd proved that opening with a grandiose statement would create tremendous resistance. Now I asked the audience if they'd let me try my intro a different way.

I put up the picture of Katy Perry again.

"I'd like to introduce you to one of my friends, Katy Perry. I know you know her and her music, but there was a lot about her career I didn't realize till I spent some time with her . . ."

Then I told a short story about Katy's career and proceeded to bullet-point out some simple facts, one by one:

- First female to have five number one hits on one album
- Which is a record that's second only to Michael Jackson's
- First artist to have multiple billion-view videos
- Eight Guinness World Records
- Record for most streamed single
- Record for sixty-nine consecutive weeks at number one

- Record for eighteen consecutive number one hits
  (no one is even close)
- One of the top-selling female artists, over 100
  million records
- Highest-grossing female artist six times

I turned to the audience. "You know what I'm going to say next, don't you?"

I walked straight over to Jamilla. "Do I even need to say it?" She just smiled and gave me a little fist bump.

"Just think about how much closer you are to my statement now."

Don't state and prove. **Inform and lead.**

I love this part. If you've found your hook, you are starting to feel your story come to life. I know that feeling; it's intoxicating. You probably want to run out and try it on everyone around.

But wait. Because there's more, and it gets even better. You've got your hook; now we want to find your **EDGE**.

Your edge is something your audience wouldn't see coming.

CHAPTER 9

THE EDGE

THE BUTT FUNNEL

If you know what a Butt Funnel is, either you're a fan of one of my TV shows or I have to wonder what kind of person you are or what college you went to.

Just kidding. It's not what it sounds like.

It's an idea that comes from the hit TV series *Bar Rescue*, starring Jon Taffer, which I created and sold in 2011. That show has aired nearly two hundred episodes now and has generated close to a quarter of a billion dollars in revenue. It is easily one of my most successful TV shows and is without a shred of doubt the best example of using what I call the edge to perfection in a pitch. The edge we used in the pitch for *Bar Rescue* was the idea of the Butt Funnel.

The first time I saw Jon Taffer was on the buzz DVD his manager sent me. All in all, he came across as big, loud, slightly obnoxious, and very impressive. Jon was a bar and nightclub owner and consultant who had made a sizable living and reputation rehabbing bars and nightclubs.

I was intrigued, but I told Jon's manager that I wanted to think about it a little. The truth was, Jon was so different that I didn't know if he was going to be likable enough for TV. I just wasn't sure. He had Gordon Ramsay's brash style going for him, but without the English accent or the sophistication of being a gourmet chef.

I called a friend who ran programming for Spike TV to ask his opinion. I didn't really want to spend the time and money chasing down a deal and developing a show if others felt the way I did.

It turned out the network loved Jon. "He is amazing. Develop something around him and bring him in for a meeting," my friend said.

So I got in touch with Jon's manager and set up a meeting, but I was still a bit skeptical. I had been through this process one hundred times with talent the network "loves," and ninety-eight of those meetings resulted in a pass. I knew that love from a network didn't always translate into a deal. I really needed to create something with Jon that would elevate him to "must have" level.

Jon and I developed the show for the network pitch meeting. The general idea was that each week, Jon would take a struggling bar, tear it to pieces, build it back up, and turn it all around. It was going to be driven by his ballsy, confrontational style and the big transformations that he helped bar owners achieve.

There was just one problem. *Kitchen Nightmares* was already a hit show, with Gordon Ramsay doing this for restaurants. We needed something more. We had the concept for the show, and Jon's fiery style was definitely the hook, but it needed some oomph. Something that would give it . . . an **edge**.

What was that going to be? The Butt Funnel. When Jon told me about the Butt Funnel, I knew we had the edge we needed for our TV show.

On the day of our pitch to the network, Jon and I entered a large conference room at the Viacom offices, where the network heads had gathered to hear our pitch

We followed the WHAC structure to deliver a crisp, clear pitch in under three minutes.

Once we had established the what and the how, we leaned in to the hook of Jon being as passionate and knowledgeable about bars as Gordon Ramsay is about restaurants, or Simon Cowell is about music. And just like Gordon and Simon, he may be loud, mean, and confrontational, but he knows his stuff and he's always right.

Then we went into the edge of the pitch.

Jon explained that during his years of bar and nightclub consulting he'd learned things about what made bars and restaurants successful that nobody talked about. While a restaurant's success largely depends on the food, clubs and bars are much different.

"Why are some clubs popular and some clubs failures?" Jon asked. "They could be next door to each other and have completely different results. I know why, and I can tell you why, every time."

The network executives all leaned in, eager to hear what Jon's secret was. Some of these executives no doubt had their own investments in the fiercely competitive New York night-club scene, and would put any advice Jon gave them to immediate use.

"Here's one thing no one else will tell you," Jon continued. "Your bar needs a Butt Funnel."

This led to some furrowed brows and head scratching from the gathered executives. *What's a Butt Funnel?* I could see them wondering.

"Every bar or nightclub has a flow or traffic pattern for people to walk around the location. People in a bar move around and survey the scene. They want to see what's going on, they want to see who's there. That creates a basic loop that people continually follow. Every time I work with a new bar, I redesign their space so this loop forms a Butt Funnel. A Butt Funnel is a spot in the bar too narrow for two people to walk through side by side. If one is coming one way and another is coming the other way, they have to turn sideways to pass each other, touching butts as they go by. When people touch butts, it sets off endorphins, men and women touching each other and initiating this contact, which imprints on people. People with a higher level of endorphins have a better time, they stay longer, they order more drinks, they spend more, they come back more often. The bar makes more money. You literally funnel the people to a spot where they have to touch butts to get through."

Jon sat down, and I could see the amazed expression on the executives' faces. I knew in that moment that we'd sold the show.

The Butt Funnel did the trick.

They bought the show. We made the show. The Butt Funnel was in episode one.

The Butt Funnel was the edge. The edge is something that cuts through the simplicity of your pitch and reminds your audience that you have something special to offer. You can also describe it as the factor that helps push it over the edge.

The edge is a cool fact or anecdote that makes someone metaphorically (and sometimes literally) sit up and take notice.

If your hook is something cool, the audience should almost know by the time they hear it that your edge is something cool they hadn't thought of before.

If you look at the Butt Funnel story, you'll see that it helps to illustrate the major statements of interest and value, but wouldn't be one on its own. It's a great example, obviously, but more than that, it forces your audience to see the context and visualize your most valuable statements.

In the *Bar Rescue* pitch, I needed to draw the buyer to the fact that Jon isn't just a loud, mean, screaming jerk. He is an expert, with years of knowledge and immense passion for the industry. He was going to share with the audience secrets that they had never heard before. Many elements inside a nightclub or bar that you thought were just random choices are really based on science. If you watch the show, you know what I'm talking about. We have this type of informative detail in every episode.

Funnily enough, when we were bullet-pointing Jon's show, we didn't have one that said "Butt Funnel," but it was so effective that I now use it as a category header with all my clients. The question is always: "What's your Butt Funnel?"

WHAT'S YOUR BUTT FUNNEL?

So what is your Butt Funnel? What story or example best illustrates your hook? Can you find that one anecdote that's just a little different to really drive the point home?

For Paraag and the WrestleMania pitch, the edge was the fact that their new app would also give everyone in the stadium real-time updates on the bathroom lines. Every bathroom and its location is mapped out on the app, and a green, yellow, and red light indicator lets the audience know exactly which bathrooms have the longest lines. Paraag and the team couldn't believe how popular this feature had become. Fans could judge the exact time when they could get to the bathroom and back to miss the least amount of the football game. The fans wouldn't miss WrestleMania matches waiting in line for the bathroom.

For Jeff and his plumbing company, the edge was a story about the hotel that hired him to re-pipe every room without disrupting the guests or alerting them that construction was going on. They didn't want to close the hotel to re-pipe it, like every other company had proposed. Jeff's guys booked a different room each night and re-piped it with no noise or mess. They went through all eighty-seven rooms without a single guest knowing they were there. They didn't wear their coveralls in the lobby or hallways: they would change in the room and walk outside in street clothes looking like guests.

Your edge is a story that has a little oomph to it, one that you can justifiably end with "Isn't that crazy?"

"People almost use the app as a game. They wait for the green light and then see how fast they can get back to their seats. They love finding bathrooms on different levels or sections with no lines. Crazy, right?"

"My guys were dressed like tourists walking through the lobby, and then they'd get into the rooms and put their work clothes on. I've never seen anything like it."

Look at your information. What's the "Can you believe it?" item? Scour your statements and your hook. Create that moment in your head that best illustrates those statements. Which one is the most dynamic, short, sweet, and kind of cool? What's your Butt Funnel?

The edge doesn't always have to be something that already happened. It can be something you think will happen or that you picture happening. When I work with startups pitching for funding, they often don't have stories of how their app works or how the product will sell because their app or product is still in its nascent stages. I help them find their edge in the potential of their product, or tell a story that explains why they saw a need for their product in the first place.

I worked with a start-up app called Bed and Bale. It's basically Airbnb for horses. Everyone who travels with a horse can go on the app and find every service in the area at their fingertips.

The idea for Bed and Bale came from an incredible story of how Virginia, the founder, had once been towing her horses when her truck blew an axle and got stuck on the side of the road. Virginia was scheduled to be at a jump competition the next morning and she was still two hundred miles away. After a few hours, she got a tow truck to come and tow the trailer, but the horses were freaking out so much that she had to take them out of the trailer and try to keep them calm. Six hours later, there was no way to get the trailer fixed and still get to the competition in time.

She had to sleep in the truck with the horses tied to the side of the trailer in a parking lot. She used Google to find places to stay, but everything suitable was closed. She knew there had to be hundreds of people in the area who owned horse trailers and had stalls available—but she had no way to find them at 11:30 p.m. If only there were an app that could connect her to someone with a trailer to rent or a stall to stay in with one click.

The edge of Virginia's pitch was that, though she didn't know it at the time, the competition she had just missed could have been a huge opportunity. The top two horses had dropped out that week, so she would've had one of her best chances to get on the podium. She consistently placed fourth or fifth, but with those two out she could have gotten third. When she eventually found out what she'd missed, it made her so frustrated that she decided to create the app she wished she'd had when she was trying to sleep in a parking lot.

The story explains the value of the app, but the added bite of her almost-podium finish gives it the edge. It makes you listen a little more carefully.

The temptation will always be to use your hook and your edge early in the pitch because they feel good and have impact. It's important to resist that temptation. There is so much more power in letting the information do the work and then using these pieces to capitalize on the situation. Inform and lead, don't state and prove.

A lot of my clients want to open their pitch with the story that should be their edge.

Conventional wisdom says to open with the problem you are solving, and I totally agree. But what we are going to work on now is using an opening to *illustrate* the problem without *stating it* directly.

It's much stronger to set up your pitch or presentation in a way that has your audience seeing the problem *before you state* it. You actually want them to have formed the solution before you even offer it.

Now we are going to work on the opening and the setup of your pitch, and get to what we talk about in TV and film as the "reason for being."

CHAPTER 10

USE YOUR NEGATIVES

I strode into the restaurant and told the hostess proudly, "I have a reservation for two under Bon Jovi."

"Yes, sir, right this way, he's waiting."

That's right, a table for two with the one and only Jon Bon Jovi, and he was already there, waiting.

I had met with Jon four or five times before in New York and LA, as we were developing a TV show together. Until now, these meetings had been at arm's length, with managers and other producers involved, so it was all business. So I was a little surprised when Jon asked to meet me over breakfast. But who's going to question the chance to get a one-on-one with maybe the greatest rock star of all time?

Two weeks earlier, Jon had left me a message to call him. When I called him back, I could hear the sound of a guitar, so I asked him, "What are you up to? Some cool rock star stuff?" He chuckled. "No, I'm practicing my scales." Jon Bon Jovi was practicing scales! That's the kind of guy he is, meticulous and disciplined.

It was only a couple of weeks before we were supposed to pitch the networks with the show we were developing, so I wasn't surprised to hear that he wanted to meet and discuss the show. I assumed he wanted to dig in some more on the pitch and rehearse a little. Jon told me he was going to be in LA early, so we planned to meet over breakfast and discuss.

Jon and I had been working on a show called *If I Wasn't a Rock Star*. The idea was that each week we'd take a famous music star and explore what their life might be like if they *hadn't* become famous in music. The star would spend a week doing the job they might have had if music hadn't worked out for them, and live with a family more in line with the life they might have had. It was a really fun idea that was getting a lot of buzz around town ever since a trade paper had broken the story that we were developing a show together.

At the time Jon and I met for breakfast, the show was ready to go out to the networks. We had been back and forth on the pitch, and meetings were set.

We met, we ordered, we chitchatted. It was kind of surreal because every few minutes someone would walk by and I knew they recognized him, and then I pictured them thinking, "Who is that guy having breakfast with Bon Jovi?" And in my mind, I was thinking, "That's right. Just me and Jon Bon Jovi, that's how I roll!"

That balloon burst when, after our initial pleasantries, Jon said, "We have a problem with the show and I can't get over it. We've built this entire premise and idea around what I would be if I *wasn't* in music, and the truth is, there is no version of me without doing music. It's all I've done and all I would ever have done. Right now we're talking about me being a landscaper because I like the outdoors. I wouldn't be a fucking landscaper, I don't like getting dirty; I've never worked outside or had a physical labor job in my life!"

Oh, crap.

Jon was right. We had built the show around the theory of what would be a cool/funny job to see huge stars like Jon doing. We were not trying to be literal with it, but Jon just couldn't get over the concept that we were selling the idea that this could have actually been his job or life. Because in his mind, he knew 100 percent it couldn't have been

"Look, I've talked to a dozen of my friends that we want for the show, and they all basically say the same thing. Music has always been their lives. Yes, they maybe had odd jobs, but I never truly would be doing anything else but music. For me and everyone else we're talking about, there was really no other option. Ever."

I already knew this. I had known it when we were developing the show. We had been pushing this landscaper idea on him, and I had sensed that he was reluctant. But I was trying to do what I thought was best for selling the concept of the show.

What Jon had brought to light at breakfast was actually a very common issue. Every new TV show idea has a problem. No idea, pitch opportunity, or presentation is perfect. There is always something that you worry the audience will fixate on, and it will suck the life out of the idea.

That two-hour breakfast with Jon Bon Jovi taught me a hugely valuable lesson that I teach all my clients and speak about in my core pitch strategy.

There's always a problem.

WHAT DO YOU HOPE THE AUDIENCE
DOESN'T FIND OUT?

When I'm working with someone or speaking, I always say, "Let's identify the problem." Without fail, everyone thinks I'm referring to the problem that their product or service is solving for the audience. And I get it. That's been the benchmark for pitching and selling since the dawn of time. You identify a problem, and then you show how your product or service solves that problem or need.

But when I talk about identifying the problem, I'm talking about identifying the problem with *your* offering.

One of the first and most powerful questions I ask every new client or audience is: "What do you hope the audience doesn't find out?"

The answers are always very telling. If people are being honest, there is something that pops to mind.

I go through this exercise because up to this point all you've been focusing on is the "value" and the "good." You've been identifying and sorting only the strongest and most impactful information to build your story and lead your audience. When we're in pitching or presenting mode, our minds are trained and conditioned to present the best and brightest and most optimistic and enthusiastic side.

That might have been good enough once. But today, it's equally as important to look at the other side of the coin. As I mentioned earlier, today's audience is overexposed to marketing and inherently skeptical. The second you start giving off the "too good to be true" vibe, their Spidey-sense starts tingling.

Just like the state-and-prove impulse causes your audience to look to disprove your statements, if your pitch or proposal is all positive and upside, your audience will look for issues and problems to balance. What's really scary is that most of the time they'll do that *while* you are presenting.

Now, you may be one of the few people on earth who has only upside to sell, and at the end of the day it doesn't matter if the audience is looking for issues. But is that really the strongest foundation to be presenting from?

No. Clearly. (And it's almost never really the case.)

You don't want your audience looking for problems or issues. You don't want their minds working against you while you explain all the benefits and potential of your fantastic idea. But if it's all sunshine and roses, that's what happens.

Have you ever made a presentation or pitch and the *very* first question is about something negative? You know, where your audience asks you the "What about X?" question the second you're done?

The truth is, if you *can* get "what about" questions, you are *going* to get them. Think about it. If the first question someone asks is about a potential issue they need you to clarify, it means they've been thinking about that issue while you've been presenting, and probably missed the value in most of what you said. You want to avoid that.

But "what about" questions don't have to be a bad thing. If you can identify them in advance, I'll show you how to use them to your advantage.

First, ask yourself the questions below to help identify your "what about":

What do you hope your audience doesn't start thinking?

What conclusion would you want them to stay away from?

What issue will they think you've overlooked?

What's the last thing you want them to ask about?

If someone says no, what would be their best reason?

If your competitor were here, what would they say about you?

If this were a debate, what would the other side be saying?

You get it. Identify the problem. Your problem.

PITCHIN' ON A PRAYER

Jon Bon Jovi was smacking me in the face with his "what about." There was no way around it. He was right. I was planning on doing what I usually did in these situations: hit the gas full throttle and power right through the issue. In the past, I'd always managed to win over the network buyers with the potential and opportunity of the show and deal with the "what about" later.

But this was going to be different. I didn't have a choice here. I needed Jon in the room the next week to speak about what he'd be doing if he wasn't a rock star. Jon was signed on to executive produce the series and he was going to star in the pilot, so this was something I had to deal with before we got into the room. I knew there was no way Jon Bon Jovi was going to go into those meetings and pitch something he didn't believe in.

Looking back, this seems even more obvious. Why would I try to force this through? Why was I hoping to hide this fact from the buyers? I'd pitched thousands of shows, so I knew for a fact that buyers were going to ask about how authentic these journeys were going to be. It's their job to ask those kinds of questions. I knew that. And yet, until Jon brought it up, I'd fooled myself into believing we could just dodge those questions.

So at that breakfast with Jon, I decided to take a different tack. "Let's just put it out there," I said. Jon was a little confused.

I said, "Let's just put it out there that there really wasn't any other option and you've never thought of any other possibility until this very moment. We will incorporate this doubt right into the pitch."

"But doesn't that take away from the very idea?" Jon asked. "I mean we're saying Lenny Kravitz would have joined the military, but actually he started playing drums at three years old and has never done anything but music."

"Not really," I replied. "Not if we own it. Not if we incorporate it into the fabric of the pitch itself. Lenny's dad was a Green Beret, so it's possible. We just need to adjust how we present it so we own the issue and the issue doesn't own us."

"Yes, but it really wasn't a possibility for Lenny," Jon said. "We really can't have a bunch of celebrities doing these jobs and basically saying, 'I would have never done this job, and thank God because this just showed me how much being a regular person sucks.'"

"Very good point," I conceded. "So let's just go in with that as an obstacle we're going to have to address and talk through."

I had no idea at the time, but this was a major breakthrough.

It felt like a subtle change then, and nothing much changed about the show that we pitched. But we planned to address the elephant in the room as part of the pitch and part of the concept.

On the big day, we roamed across Los Angeles pitching the show to all the network and cable buyers. We explained how most of these music stars never considered other jobs, but we were going to force them to explore the possibility. At every network I noticed this becoming a stronger point and helping the overall pitch. So I started embracing it to a fuller extent.

I said to ABC, "It would be amazing if we could find stars that had real jobs and had to make a real choice between music and their other career. But so far, we haven't found that. Performers at the level we're casting for the show are like Jon. They've never had a shred of doubt about music being their life's calling and their only option. Our big concern is that because they've never really considered other careers, it may come off as 'look how crappy regular people have it.'"

The head of ABC responded before I could continue. "Yes, of course, but it will be fascinating to see Jon and other stars forced to consider the alternative universe. And they'll find things about regular jobs and family life that they haven't experienced with their crazy travel lives. I think if it's done right, those could be very heartfelt moments."

We were definitely onto something.

We ended up with four offers on the show, so the pitch worked. Would it have worked without this change? Maybe.

But I've had home run ideas before that struck out in a meeting because "problems" took over the pitch and we weren't prepared for them. I'm not sure Jon would have been comfortable if a meeting unfolded that way, and that discomfort may have given the wrong message.

Hard to say how things would have played out if Jon hadn't asked me to breakfast that day. But what's not hard to say is that experience changed every pitch I'd ever make from that day forward. It was a great lesson.

Thank you, JBJ!

Jon Bon Jovi and yours truly,
right after we pitched ABC

(If you're wondering why you've never seen this show on TV, it's because we couldn't get out of the deal phase with the network and our other partner, the Weinstein Company. After many attempts there were just too many mouths to feed and too many egos at work. Welcome to the wonderful world of television.)

USING A WEAKNESS AS A STRENGTH

I realized going through the Jon Bon Jovi pitch that I had been able to use the weakness in the show as a strength. I noticed I was using the potential downside as a way to inject and validate a more important upside.

In any celebrity-based show, there is always the giant concern about casting. Can you actually get celebrities to show up, and can you get *real* celebrities to show up? It's not enough to just say to the buyer, "Hey, we're going to get big-name celebrities."

In this pitch, we were saying, "We haven't found any celebrity to cast that had a real job yet. They've always known music was their life. So far, all of Jon's friends who are interested in the show are at levels like that."

The concern was that it might come across as if the stars were looking down on regular people when they really weren't.

By saying all this up front in this fashion I was able to validate that:

1. We've already been talking to and casting celebrities.
2. We're obviously talking to big stars who are big enough to be in music from the start.
3. The level of commitment from Jon Bon Jovi is serious because he's been out there with us researching and talking to his star friends.
4. We've really thought this through and we're being straight about what we can deliver.
5. We are thinking about and addressing potential creative issues with the network, we are so confident in our ability to bring them into the process.

I could clearly feel how effective this was in the pitch. I knew it the second we walked out of the room at ABC.

I started to use my negatives to accentuate and validate the positives from that moment on, and I'll show you how to do it in your pitch or presentation.

I went back and assembled my development team and asked them to bring in our slate of show ideas. I then went around the room and tried to find the "problem" with each of them.

Not surprisingly, it didn't take more than a minute for each show. Everyone knew these issues. My team had been thinking about them since the moment we crafted the pitches, but nobody was talking about them. Our plan was always to power through them and overwhelm the issues with positive and compelling information.

"If you were the buyer, why would you pass on this show?" I asked for each idea on the slate. "OK, so let's talk about it in the room, let's get right into it."

From that moment on, part of our development process was to identify the biggest negative issues and bring them into the pitch before the network executives had a chance to get them in their minds.

I decided I was going to be the one to bring up the potential issues or questions about the format. I wanted the network buyers to be the ones defending the merits of the idea, not me.

In a pitch on a big competition show to NBC, I said, "I'm not sure we can actually cast this show. The window will be very narrow and our goals might be too specific, and without the right cast, I'm not sure the show even works."

The response in the room from the network was "We always find a cast, and we can open it up wider if needed. Even with just a 'good' cast it makes for some real drama."

I couldn't have said it any better myself, and it was so much more powerful that I didn't have to!

I once sold a show to ABC called *Celebrity Splash*, about celebrities learning to dive off an Olympic diving tower. Go ahead and laugh. Believe me, it sounded just as ridiculous then as it does now. But I knew that when we were pitching it. So I embraced it in the pitch.

I said in and as part of the pitch, "We'll try for a big-name celebrity cast, but there is no way A-list celebrities are going to do it, so we have to accept that. That's going to mean there is a real chance the audience thinks this is as ridiculous as we do. You know as well as I do that just because it was a massive hit in Europe doesn't mean it will work here. It may just be too silly."

Sure enough, John Saade, the head of ABC, was saying, "Yes, but I think that's the appeal of it. We have to play into the absurdity and camp of it. That's what makes it a spectacle. I think that's why it worked so well in Europe."

Can you see it?

Can you see how my audience was starting to solve my problem for me? Can you see how I would use my setup and the valuable and compelling elements of the pitch to give my audience the ability to solve my problem for me?

How much more powerful is that than trying to hide the problem and having the buyers at ABC saying after the pitch, "I can't imagine you'll get real celebrities." I was able to reinforce what a hit show it was in Europe without simply stating it again.

THE "ALL IS LOST" MOMENT

This works on the same principle as a crucial Hollywood storytelling technique called the "all is lost" moment.

This is the moment in the film where everything goes wrong and the hero has nothing left to lose. It's used to get the audience to anticipate and desire a big turnaround and the eventual happy, or happier, ending.

When you see the bad guy almost winning, when it looks like all is lost, you want that retribution, you want that moment to turn around. You are begging for the hero to pop back to life.

In the *Rocky* movies, it's the moment when it looks like he's down for the count. You are almost yelling at the screen, "Get up!" The writer has created this moment so you anticipate and desire what happens next. Rocky gets up. And you as the audience are drawn deeper into the character, and now you truly believe and support his mission.

You don't see this sort of moment and think, "Oh, that's it, life is so bad in Shawshank Prison I just want Andy Dufresne [Tim Robbins] to wither and die quietly." Nope. You *want* him to escape. You know exactly why you want him to escape, because the previous eighty minutes made you root for him and hate what he's going through. You believe in his journey.

By creating a small "all is lost" moment in your story or pitch, you create a rooting interest for your audience. You create that moment where they look to believe in your story. I tell everyone I work with that there are only three options with potential downsides or negatives:

A. You bring up the negative and let your audience look to solve it.
B. You wait until your audience brings up the negative and then you try to address it.
C. Nobody brings up the negative, the audience believes it, and nobody solves or addresses it.

Which do you think is the more powerful strategy?

A, right?

By the way, there is no option D, where the audience doesn't notice or think of the negative. In today's world, your audience is picking apart every statement and is always poised to find the downside. They will just assume you're trying to hide it.

That's the other risk/reward to this equation. It gives a very distinct impression of you and the way you're perceived.

YOUR AUDIENCE WILL HATE YOU
FOR HIDING THE NEGATIVE

I once worked with a biotech company that had a very small irregularity in their financial model concerning their debt load. It didn't look great, but in reality it wasn't a huge issue. It also had nothing to do with the product or research and the potential for the company. I watched their investor presentation, and sure enough the second the CEO opened up for questions, he got peppered with inquiries about the debt and the way it was structured.

That made the CEO uncomfortable and slightly annoyed. His answers were a little dismissive and not all that thorough. So the next question from the audience was more of the same, and so on. He took eleven different questions about his financing and debt before anybody asked him about the great new migraine drug that was the whole point of his presentation.

I'm no financial genius, but even I knew the debt issue was minor in the scheme of things and was nowhere near as important as the medical breakthrough they were making. But when I talked to a couple of the investor representatives outside the meeting, many of them said things like "I don't trust him," or "There's probably stuff going on behind the scenes he's not telling us," and so on.

I bet you've seen this on *Shark Tank*. Mark Cuban (he does this the most) asks a question about something barely related to the pitch, and it opens up a Pandora's box. The magic in the show is the editing, because it always looks like Mark pulled this question out of nowhere and caught the entrepreneur off guard. What really happens is that there is a very long question-and-answer session that goes on during the filming that doesn't make the final cut. Mark is always looking for the "What are they not telling me?"

I once worked on a really fun TV project with Mark, and he told me, "The money is not important to me, it's the people. And if I can find them hiding info or trying to avoid telling me something negative, that's not a partner I want."

Unfortunately, what the biotech CEO had done was give the impression that he was purposely avoiding the issue. I knew he wasn't, he just didn't believe it had real relevance. He was so passionate about his work and about how valuable it was that he thought discussing this simple financial bump that could be fixed with his next round of funding was a waste of time. I'll say that he actually was one of the lucky ones. Being the CEO of a public company comes with some serious disclosure requirements, so he was obligated to show this information to his audience no matter what. That's the way the public company sphere rolls. If he wasn't required to disclose this issue, I can guarantee that he wouldn't have mentioned it once, and that would have been worse. Because every investor who seriously looked at the details of his company was eventually going to see it.

If they saw it later, they would have assumed he was trying to bury it. The audience doesn't like it when you gloss over the negative, but they despise it if you try to hide it. Whether you are trying to hide it or not, if they think you've avoided something on purpose, it sends screaming shock waves through their system. They distrust everything about anything you've said to or shown them.

I asked the CEO to try bringing up this debt issue and talk it through in the first three minutes. I wanted him to get those questions zapped before they got into someone's head. He was reluctant, but I showed him how he could use that moment to explain the company's conservative fiscal policy and how it was costing them in the short term but that now they were ready to move to the next phase. This was in keeping with the core values of their company.

I promised him he wouldn't get a lot of probing questions when he opened up the floor. The first question was, in fact, a question about the financing on the debt. But this time it was an investor asking the CEO if they'd be interested in investment and a loan refinance from the questioner's group! It was a 180-degree turnaround from the questions he had gotten before. This investor saw it as an opportunity, not a negative. And now nobody saw it as something he was hiding or trying to avoid.

So take your answers to "What do I hope my audience doesn't find out?" and identify the one that stands out as a potential issue. Now look to your statements of interest and find the ones that could validate why this problem isn't such a problem. I call these your props (because they prop up your issue).

The best way to do this is to picture your audience asking the question you don't want them to ask. What elements of the pitch would you use to defend yourself? Which of your statements of interest counteract it the best?

Most likely you are taking these from your facts, figures, logic, and reason category of the "Are you sure?" section of the WHAC system. It's the part of your pitch where you are going to verify and validate what it is and how it works, so it's the perfect opportunity to address those issues that you will show are not actually issues.

If you think back to the pitch for WrestleMania, the negative was that the stadium was brand new. Yes, that's shiny and cool, but new stadiums have growing pains. Growing pains with nearly ninety thousand fans are not cool.

So there was no way that Vince McMahon wouldn't be thinking this. It made no sense not to bring it up. So Paraag explained while he was talking about the size and scope of the arena that there had been some growing pains with launching the stadium. He told stories of chaos, issues, and unforeseen problems.

Of course Vince McMahon knows that a nearly $2 billion stadium that hosts one of the greatest NFL franchises and some of the biggest events in the world is going to do whatever is necessary to make things run smoothly. But because Paraag preemptively addressed these issues, it eliminated any potential concerns Vince might have had in this area. Not only that, it gave Paraag the chance to reiterate in a more detailed way that this stadium has the best infrastructure and is the most technologically advanced.

So find your moment and work the negatives into your presentation with "We were surprised to learn," or "I still struggle with," or "What we are trying to avoid," or "The problem we're working through," or "My initial concerns were" whenever appropriate.

It's an easy and effective tool. Don't be afraid to use it. Don't be afraid to really dig in. You almost can't go too far. If the negatives were really a deal breaker, you wouldn't still be pursuing the idea. You must believe in the upside enough for it to outweigh the problem. So you need to trust that if you make your audience see things the way you do, they'll agree.

I make all my private clients do this exercise. Sometimes, their list of negatives is totally phony and contrived, as if they're giving a canned response to the interview question "What don't you do well, what's your weakness, in what areas do you need improvement?"

Every time I hear something like "I work too hard" or "I'm a chronic overachiever," my brain says, "Bullshit," and it makes that person harder to hire.

There is a clear confidence in using your weaknesses that absolutely shines through when you admit them without fear or spin. It screams to the audience that you believe in your business, product, or service so deeply that the downside is not an issue and can be addressed anytime for any reason.

OK, are you ready to put it all together?

So far, we've got your statements of interest, we've identified your hook, we've found the story that will give you the edge, we've got your story laid out in WHAC order, and we've identified the negative you can prop up.

Let me show you how we build a pitch from scratch so you can see exactly how to use all these methods and test your pitch in the real world.

CHAPTER 11

YOUR 3-MINUTE PITCH

As I began writing this chapter, I learned that a friend and client just closed a $10 million financing round for his new app. Since he and I recently finished putting together his 3-Minute pitch, and I love when things work out so beautifully, I want to walk you through how we built it from scratch, so you can follow along to see how to build yours.

The idea was for a new app called Freebird. It's a simple idea with a lot of moving parts.

Here is how it came to life:

Kurt Brendlinger was in my office, grinning from ear to ear. He had an idea for an app. He had spent the little money he had on developing it, and he was committed to making it a reality.

He had a very detailed deck and walked me through it. It was overloaded with facts and figures and options and technical jargon. When Kurt finished, I could see the excitement on his face. He thought it was clear as a bell and I would be jumping for joy with him.

It wasn't and I wasn't. Not yet.

But I dug into it with him and dissected what it really was and how it worked. Once I could see it, I got excited. I asked him to explain where he got the idea.

Kurt had come up with the idea for Freebird while asking for dinner suggestions from a waitress at the golf course. When she suggested three places in town, Kurt asked, "Which one is your favorite?"

She replied, "I like Jester's."

"Why Jester's?" he asked.

"Because they pay for my Uber."

That was the spark. That's what Kurt had developed. A ride service amenity for restaurants and bars.

Kurt had a basic idea for how the app worked, he had run some tests, and he had created some models. He had done his research and done everything he could do on his own. Now he needed to raise money.

I gladly agreed to help him build his presentation.

We began with the Post-it notes and the whiteboard. I'm literally copying from my office board notes.

BULLETS

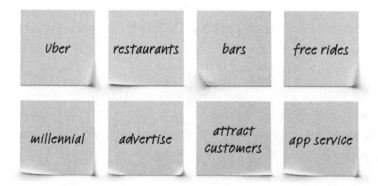

credit cards	reimburse-ments	open source	area specific
paying customers	drinking	groups	safety
ride share	information tracking	credits	behavior
ride budget	prizes and incentives	area radius	captive audience
self-contained	all rides	brands	direct marketing
increase bar tabs	any service		

Once we had the bullets, we started to form our statements.

STATEMENTS

- Uber—Uber and Lyft do millions of rides each night
- Restaurants—people take Uber out for the night
- Bars—people take Uber to bars so they don't have to drive home
- Free rides—bars/restaurants offer free rides to potential customers
- Millennial—use Uber service more than anyone
- Advertise—bars and restaurants can advertise to potential clients
- Attract customers—offer free rides to bring in potential customers
- App service—all done through the app
- Credit cards—we track credit card purchases
- Reimbursements—they get their ride money back after purchase
- Open source—Uber and Lyft opened their code
- Area specific—bars can set where to draw customers
- Paying customers—customers must spend money in bar to get free ride
- Drinking—people drink more when they don't drive
- Groups—attract groups of friends sharing Uber
- Safety—encourage more people to use service if free
- Ride share—everyone going out for the night considers using Uber or Lyft
- Information tracking—we know who goes where and what they spend
- Credits—we give prizes for using service

- Behavior—customer must purchase to get free ride
- Ride budget—bars can set a budget per ride
- Prizes and incentives—we give sponsor prizes for all rides
- Area radius—the radius area determines the budget
- Captive audience—they are in ride for duration
- Self-contained—the app hails and pays for Uber directly
- All rides—not just sponsor rides earn credits
- Brands—other advertisers can market or give prizes
- Direct marketing—the app delivers direct to customer
- Increase bar tabs—when people take Uber to a bar, they drink and spend more
- Any service—doesn't matter Uber or Lyft or taxi or something new; all work

Next, we put them into our buckets:

INFORMATION

Uber—Uber and Lyft do millions of rides each night

Restaurants—people take Uber out for the night

Bars—people take Uber to bars so they don't have to drive home

Free rides—we offer free rides to sponsor bars

Advertise—bars and restaurants can advertise to potential clients

Attract customers—offer free rides to bring in potential customers

App service—all done through the app

Reimbursements—they get their ride money back after purchase

Paying customers—customers must spend money in bar to get free ride

Ride budget—bars can set a budget per ride

Prizes and incentives—we give sponsor prizes for all rides

Area radius—the radius area determines the budget

Behavior—customer must act according to promise

Self-contained—the app hails and pays for Uber directly

ENGAGEMENT

Millennial—use Uber service more than anyone

Credit cards—we track credit card purchases

Open source—Uber and Lyft opened their code

Area specific—bars can target where to draw customers

Drinking—people drink more when they don't drive

Groups—attract groups of friends sharing Uber

Safety—encourage more people to use service if free

Ride share—everyone going out for the night considers using Uber or Lyft

Information tracking—we know who goes where and what they spend

Credits—we give prizes for using service

Captive audience—they are in ride for duration

All rides—not just sponsor rides earn credits

Brands—other advertisers can market or give prizes

Direct marketing—the app delivers direct to customer

Increase bar tabs—when people take Uber to a bar, they drink and spend more

Any service—doesn't matter Uber or Lyft or taxi or something new; all work

BEFORES AND AFTERS

Next, we did some befores and afters to organize the flow.

Restaurants—people take Uber out for the night

Bars—people take Uber to bars so they don't have to drive home

Uber—Uber and Lyft do millions of rides each night

Free rides—bars/restaurants offer free rides to potential customers

Attract customers—offer free rides to bring in potential customers

App service—all done through the app

Self-contained—the app hails and pays for Uber directly

Paying customers—customers must spend money in bar to get free ride

Reimbursements—they get their ride money back after purchase

Behavior—customer must purchase to get free ride

Ride budget—bars can set a budget per ride

Area radius—the radius area determines the budget

Prizes and incentives—we give sponsor prizes for all rides

Advertise—bars and restaurants can advertise to potential clients

Then we started to filter the core information through the WHAC process to clean it up and find the hook.

WHAT IS IT?

App that lets bars and restaurants pay for customers' Uber and Lyft rides. Bar and restaurant owners offer free rides to customers willing to come to their bar for the night. Customers open the app and see who's offering to pay for their ride. They select the spot, and if they spend money in that bar or restaurant, their ride is free. The bars and restaurants aren't paying for marketing to *potential* customers: they are spending money on *actual* paying customers.

Notice how we categorized the process of using the app as "what it is" and not in the "how it works" section, because the real question about how it works is going to be about how the app works for the bar or restaurant. The core idea is that the customer simply opens an app and gets a free ride.

HOW DOES IT WORK?

While the service is seamless for the customer, they must spend money in that bar to get the free ride. The Freebird app connects directly to the customer's Uber app, so the customer hails and pays for their Uber as they normally would. But with Freebird, the cost of the ride is tracked, and when the customer spends money at the bar or restaurant, the cost of their ride is credited back to them seamlessly. Because of this, the bar or restaurant can set a budget they want to spend on free rides, and knows that each new customer is guaranteed to spend that money in their bar or restaurant. Customers get free rides, and bars and restaurants get new paying customers. Freebird takes a commission.

ARE YOU SURE?

The app lets bars and restaurants control when and how much they spend on attracting customers by the number of free rides they offer. On days the bar or restaurant is normally very busy, they may decide to offer little or no incentive. On days they are slow, that can turn up their budget and "drive" new customers, pun intended. Research shows that customers who use a ride service like Uber spend 20 percent more on their bar and restaurant tabs than those who drive. By offering an incentive to use a ride service, the bars and restaurants will attract higher-spending customers.

CAN YOU DO IT?

Uber and Lyft both opened their API (application programming interface) structure to allow third-party apps to use their platform directly. Freebird is connected directly to the customer's Uber or Lyft account so we can track their rides and correlate them to their credit card purchases. It's seamless for the consumer to use, but allows the bar or restaurant to guarantee they only pay for rides for customers who spend money in their establishment.

Once we had the basic structure and the valuable elements in the right order, we looked at building our story and connecting each idea.

THE HOOK

As we've learned, the hook is something that your audience should be thinking about as they hear, read, or see your pitch. Freebird's hook is that the customer can only get a free ride if they first spend money in the host bar or restaurant. That was a huge distinction because the ability to ensure that the customer buys something in order to receive the free ride is crucial. That's particularly so when the average Uber ride is nine dollars and the average bar tab is twenty-six dollars.

> The hook: Freebird helps find your customer, picks them up, brings them to your location, and then ensures they spend money in your establishment to receive the free ride.

THE EDGE AND THE NEGATIVE

It was easy to define and connect the two. The negative to the idea was so big and definitive that by solving it, it pushed the idea over the edge.

Kurt used the story about how they struggled early with the idea that if they paid for someone's ride to the restaurant, there was no way to ensure that the customers actually went into that particular establishment. He talked about the early trials where customers would show up at the test restaurant to meet friends only to leave when they got there. This was a problem, as this meant that the app was effectively just a paid advertisement, where the bar would have to hope the customer spent money in their establishment.

But when they discovered their credit card scraping technology, everything changed. It allowed Freebird to scrape credit card data from the bar or restaurant to look for matches to the customer's credit card number. When it finds a match, it automatically triggers their reimbursement.

> The edge: Freebird is not in the free ride business, it is in the ride reimbursement business.

Once we had that basic structure, all the other pieces and engagement elements fell into place.

There were a lot of grand gestures and ideas that we left out because we had to trust that the audience would get there on their own. We knew that the idea of advertisers paying for transportation was big, but as you'll see in the next chapter regarding the opening and closing of a pitch, we were able to use the size and scope of the ride-sharing economy to illustrate the massive potential without trying to state and prove it.

I've posted on my website the original and complete versions of the Freebird pitch, deck, and promo video, and a video of Kurt actually pitching Freebird to a venture capital firm. It's a beautiful 3-Minute pitch and I recommend watching it. One thing to note, keep an eye on the simplicity of the slides in Kurt's PowerPoint. This will add context to the forthcoming chapter about how to use PowerPoint.

Check it out: 3minuterule.com/freebird.

Now that you've seen how the process works from scratch, go back through and finalize the 3-Minute pitch for your business or idea.

IT'S ALL ABOUT "AND THEN"

The great television writer and TV mogul Stephen J. Cannell was a dear friend of mine, and he taught me how to write a story early in my career. Even if you don't recognize the name, you know Stephen's work. He's responsible for creating some of the most iconic TV shows of all time, from *The Rockford Files* to *The A-Team*, from *21 Jump Street* to *The Greatest American Hero*. You know his signature ending with the man pulling the page out of the typewriter and it floating on down to form the *C* in Cannell Studios. Stephen was a brilliant writer and influenced some of the greatest writers in entertainment, including Steven Bochco, Dick Wolf, and David Bellisario.

Stephen's style was overly simple. That was his blessing and curse. He couldn't write edgy and subversive and subtle. That just wasn't in him. He was straight down the middle. That's why he had forty-plus TV series in his career, because a clean story with good characters always works. Yes, every now and then a show with wildly complicated twists and unexplained story lines like *Lost* becomes a hit show, but for every one of those, there are twenty *CSI*s or *NCIS*s or *Law & Order*s or *A-Team*s that run for years.

Stephen had two iron-clad rules for his successful story-telling.

The first was "Always let the audience know what the bad

guy is doing" (I'm hoping that's one you won't have to apply), and the second was "Always write with the 'and then' for each scene."

If you watch a Stephen Cannell series or read one of his twenty-two bestselling novels (which I highly recommend), you'll notice that the story flows from scene to scene like "this happened *and then* they did this *and then* they went here *and then* this was the plan *and then* . . ."

It's linear and sequential and pulls you through the story. You know how it's going to end, and you know it will resolve because he's been feeding it to you piece by piece. By the climax, even though you know how it's going to end, you are so invested in the process, you absolutely want it to end just like that. How many times have you been flipping channels on TV and found yourself getting caught up in a *CSI* episode or a *Dateline* special? They are champions of the "and then" storytelling.

DON'T TARANTINO YOUR PRESENTATION

I'm a big fan of Quentin Tarantino's *Pulp Fiction*, and maybe you are, too, but it's on an island of the few movies and TV series that have been successful after drastically breaking with this pattern. For every movie or TV show that succeeds by breaking the rules, at least one thousand find success by sticking with the pattern.

Your story, your 3-Minute pitch, is an "and then" story. Straight, linear, clear.

You want your audience to go "and then" all the way through. You *want* them to feel like they know how it will end. You want them to hope for the resolution they desire. You want *your* conclusion to be *their* conclusion.

This is how I want you to pitch and present and convey information. I want you to make the audience subconsciously say "and then" after each statement and piece of information. We are laying bread crumbs. Delicious and easy-to-follow bread crumbs.

I say this to a lot of clients: "You are not M. Night Shyamalan, this isn't *The Sixth Sense*." Don't be clever, don't be cute, don't try to build to a big reveal, don't try to misdirect and surprise, don't try to break the mold.

Maybe you're the Quentin Tarantino of pitching and presenting. It could be that you have the talent and flair to break all the norms and find success by blazing your own trail. But chances are your talents lie elsewhere; plus, finding success by breaking all the rules is a lot harder than taking the path that's tried and tested. That's why, when it comes to pitching, one of my favorite rules of thumb is "Don't try to Tarantino this."

Run through your 3-Minute pitch a few times, and when you've got it the way you want it, if you'd like, post it anonymously at 3minuterule.com/my3minutes and I'll select and critique the most illustrative ones I get on the site, so you can see and learn from everyone's experience.

THE TELEPHONE TEST

This a fun and wildly revealing test that I absolutely force people to do. If I could force you to do it, I would.

What you believe is clear and concise and easy to follow may not be that way to others.

What you may not realize about great Hollywood writers is that they are unique in their ability to make the imagery, emotion, and story clear to everyone in the same way.

What you've probably never thought of is that every person who writes a screenplay thinks it's great. The reason is, all the motivation and emotions are perfectly clear to the writer. The writer understands the characters and the twists and the story elements perfectly, as clear as a bell.

Surprise! What not all writers are good at is making the audience see their story and characters the way they do (sound familiar?). The only difference between a great script and an OK script is the ability for the reader to grasp it all as the writer intended. This should sound familiar. It's what we've been talking about on every page of this book.

Look at your 3-Minute pitch. I'm betting you feel it, know it, understand it, appreciate it, and believe in it. To you it's very clear and concise. You might even think it's a little *too* simple. So let's test that theory.

I want you to get in touch with a friend and enlist their help. Choose someone who doesn't know your pitch or presentation or maybe even what you've been working on. Ask them to listen to your pitch. Then ask them to call someone else and pitch it to them. Ask them to then pitch it one more time to a third person, who is going to call you and pitch it back to you.

You know what's going to happen, don't you?

You or your kids have probably played some form of telephone at birthday parties all your lives.

And what you're thinking should scare and excite you. I know you don't want to do this, and many of you will skip though it or pitch it to one person and ask them to pitch it back to you. But this is an amazing exercise and you should jump at the opportunity to get real feedback. If you only do three degrees of telephone on this, you will be shocked at how much information you get back. You'll also be surprised at how much information is lost in translation. There will be elements that you felt were so important that never made it down the line. That's OK, you can adjust. But you need this input.

I sat in a conference room with a company that was trying to raise money to start a network that would provide information about legal marijuana. It was a great idea to centralize the information about the laws of marijuana into one easy-to-access, all-knowing service. You have a question about weed, they have answers. They don't sell anything, they don't stock anything, they just provide the service. Think 1-800-DENTIST, but for marijuana.

I called my brother, and asked my client Keith (the weed info king) to pitch him on the phone. He did, and then I gave my brother the phone number for the conference room. "I need you to pitch that concept to one of your friends, and then have them pitch one of their friends, and then give them this number and call to pitch it back to us. Tell them it's a game and we have to have it back in one hour."

We hung up the phone and went back to work and discussed the company some more. After forty-five minutes the phone rang. You would not believe the excitement that jolted in the room. We put the conference phone on speaker.

"Hi. This is Jeffrey? I was asked to call you guys for this game and pitch this idea?" Jeffrey was a millennial. Millennials tend to end their sentences with rising voices and question marks.

"Yes, Jeffrey. Please go ahead. We are listening."

Jeffrey pitched us an idea about a weed shop that stores your information, and you can access it anytime. They have a social media service that you use to find information on specific news about the marijuana industry.

It was a mess and it wasn't at all what Keith was pitching. What was revealing was that the one piece of information that survived was the 1-800-DUI-HIGH phone number. Jeffrey knew perfectly well that that was the number to call if you had questions about the laws in your state and if you needed to connect to a lawyer who specialized in marijuana issues.

This was really helpful. It showed us what pieces of the pitch were resonating (people tend to remember the things they like or are drawn to), and it showed where some of Keith's ideas that looked clear on paper were not being understood.

We played the game a few more times (we actually had to buy $200 in Starbucks gift cards to bribe people to play after we ran out of personal connections), and eventually Keith's pitch was coming back the same way it went out. That was a very exciting call.

You might feel apprehensive. I get it. It's the feeling that I get when I screen a movie for the first time for an audience that doesn't know me. I hate it. Or when I have to fly to Vegas to do a focus group for a TV show with twelve strangers paid $25 and a sandwich to give their opinions about my show. There has been more than one time I wanted to jump through the two-way glass and strangle someone.

But it's important to face the reality of the public and the people you are pitching to. That's what you're facing, so you are way better off facing them on your terms in a practice run. I can assure you, what you learn will be well worth it.

Play the game. Make the calls. Buy the gift cards if you have to.

Do it once and you'll be hooked. Yes, it kind of sucks the first time because you'll want to scream, "How stupid are you?" when they don't pitch something back to you that is as beautiful and obvious as when it went out. But when you eventually answer the phone and a stranger pitches you back your idea and gets it right, you will scream with joy. I've seen it.

CHAPTER 12

OPENING, CALLBACK, AND ENDING

'm sitting across a chaotic desk from Jimmy Fallon, surrounded with toys and gadgets and pictures and items I can't even describe (and I thought my work space was "busy"). We are in his funky office in New York at 30 Rockefeller Center, laughing hysterically while reminiscing about Cameron Diaz, in a hammock, with forty-eight bunny rabbits.

Wait, what?

Yes, you read that correctly: Cameron Diaz, in a hammock, with forty-eight bunnies. Thanks to Jimmy Fallon.

Jimmy Fallon is an absolute master of the opening.

That's what this chapter is about.

I watched Jimmy do this opening brilliantly in a pitch meeting with NBC on a show we sold called *That's a Record*. He told the president of the network about how YouTube was changing the way he searched for comedy bits and entertainment, and then he told him all his friends were doing it as well.

He told the story of how Cameron Diaz had seen a hilarious clip of someone setting a world record for holding bunnies in a hammock.

How on earth is that a record or a thing? She couldn't get over it. So Jimmy suggested that she break that record on the show. For no reason other than Cameron Diaz would get in a hammock onstage and put forty-eight tiny cute little bunnies in there with her. So she did it.

You've seen that clip, right? If you haven't, you must (https://recordsetter.com/world-record/bunnies-snuggled -with-hammock/932)!

More important, it set up his "reason for being" (I'll explain shortly), and everyone wanted to learn about the show idea.

Jimmy explained that a radio station in Australia saw the Cameron Diaz clip and decided to beat it. That went viral, so then Jimmy brought Cameron on to beat it again. She did.

The next thing you know, all of Jimmy's celebrity friends are calling about fun YouTube clips they found and odd records or feats they want to try.

It turns out that there is an actual database, called Record-Setter (originally called the International Record Database), that keeps track of world records for anything. You just have to submit the paperwork and the proper proof, and they will catalog it.

So Jimmy started having his celebrity friends and a pair of judges from the organization on the show each week to set hilarious and fun records.

And that is how we came up with *That's a Record*.

This may look like an obvious setup, but Jimmy's story

and setup are a little more nuanced and clever than they may seem.

What Jimmy has mastered is a form of storytelling and interaction called "pre-suasion." It's the process of influencing what your audience is thinking *before* you start pitching or presenting. It's a classic Hollywood storytelling system that filmmakers and novelists use to give you a certain feeling and understanding before the story begins. It's important and powerful, and once I discovered it and started to study it, it's been a core element in every pitch and presentation or story I deliver.

I always ask in my seminars, "Why did Bambi's mom die at the beginning of the film?"

Disney could easily have told the story of Bambi just getting lost, or not shown Bambi's mom dying, or done it later in the film. But by opening with that piece, they instantly set your emotions and thoughts exactly where they need to be to get into the story of Bambi. Bambi's mom had nothing to do with the actual story. If you think of the movie, once his mom dies, Bambi's journey and the movie begin.

Take my favorite film, *Braveheart.* Yeah, yeah, just humor me here. The opening is William Wallace's dad heading out to fight the English and coming back dead. Now we are prepared to watch this young boy return and eventually claim his country.

It's pre-suasion.

The reason Jimmy Fallon is so good at it is that comedians do pre-suasion in almost every joke. They set up the scene and your thoughts on it before they deliver the punch line. A lot of comedy is done in little stories, so they master the art of pre-suasion.

When we were pitching *That's a Record*, Jimmy's intro was all about making the network buyer feel and think, "I'd like to see that." And when you're pitching a TV show, that's a pretty good feeling for the buyer to have before you start the pitch and explain the show. Jimmy told the story of Cameron Diaz with the bunnies, and how his celebrity friends wanted to do similar funny skits. That story was the intro.

So let's go back to the pitch you built in the last chapter and look at how to develop an intro that sets up your listener perfectly.

Start with asking yourself what you'd want your audience to be feeling or thinking *before* you start explaining your pitch. To help you narrow that down, always think of what they would *want* most out of the pitch. You will design an intro that gets your audience to *feel* what **they** *want*.

Remember my friend Virginia who pitched the Airbnb for horses? She knew the investors *wanted* to make money. She wanted them to *feel* that her idea could be an opportunity to make money and capture an untapped market.

In her case, the best opening to her pitch was a very quick summary of the strength and opportunity that Airbnb's explosion in popularity provided.

The key to her opening was the story of Airbnb and the problems the company had trying to get venture capitalists to understand the value when they launched. Everyone thought, "Who would want to go stay at a stranger's house?"

She then pointed out that in a few short years, the consumer is now completely comfortable with the Airbnb model. The sharing economy is now part of our culture. All thanks to Airbnb.

She's now ready to tell investors that Bed and Bale is Airbnb for horses. Her potential investor is already feeling that people *know* what Airbnb is and how it works. The consumer inherently understands—and the opportunity and structure are already established. Her story about how much work Airbnb did to build the platform and create the system both on the consumer side and the operations side established that all of the heavy lifting was already done. Now you could see. Anyone who has a horse is going to "get it" immediately.

Jimmy's opening with Cameron and the hammock and the bunnies highlighted for the TV executives that YouTube is a great source of must-see material. The insight: Jimmy and his celebrity friends can harness that.

THE REASON FOR BEING

I'm driving you toward what I call **the reason for being**. The reason for being tells the audience how you came to be involved with this idea or proposal. It's the question of why you got interested and where the idea came from, and, crucially, how you figured out the idea was good.

Think about it in a story setting. The reason for being is the setup that says, "Now you know why I'm about to tell you *this* story about *this* character." Bambi's mom is dead.

William Wallace's dad is dead. Airbnb has created the market (nobody's dead). There was a really funny YouTube clip and now we have Cameron Diaz in a hammock with bunnies.

It subtly tells the audience why they should care. And when done right it opens the audience's mind to the possibilities ahead and warms them up to the story and events that are about to unfold. It's like an opening act at a comedy show or rock concert. It prepares you for what's to come.

So you want to find your opening act.

To get started, ask yourself some of these questions:

Why am I excited about this?

When did I discover the opportunity?

What happened to make this an opportunity?

What was my first thought when I realized how this could work?

Who opened my eyes to the possibilities?

Where did I learn about this?

When was the first seed of this idea?

What surprised me when I started looking into this?

This will help you find a story that opens up your pitch and sets up your reason for being.

When I work with clients building a presentation, I always look for the reason for being that has two parts:

1. When you *thought* it was good
2. When you *verified* it was good

Part 1 is how you open and part 2 is how you "call back"—which I'll explain shortly.

In my TV pitches I do this in a very specific setup. I always use a story about a successful show and something specific I find interesting or compelling. I just sold a show that is effectively *The Amazing Race* for really smart engineering-type people who could build their way across the world.

I opened the pitch like this:

"We started studying some of the recent TV hits and noticed something very interesting about how the audience is evolving in their expectation of competition."

This tells the buyer that there is some depth to this.

"Look at what *The Voice* did to *American Idol*. *American Idol* was putting on talented amateurs, but *The Voice* was putting on the best singers to start the show. *Naked and Afraid* took *Survivor* and brought in experts. With *American Ninja Warrior*, it's just *Wipeout* with experts doing a harder obstacle course.

"The audience is evolving, wanting to see aspirational competition. We realized that nobody had done this for *The Amazing Race*. They've had thirty seasons of hapless nitwits struggling to find their way around the world. Well, it's time to up the game and bring in the experts. It's called *The Mad Dash*."

My less-than-thirty-second intro neatly explains why we came up with this show.

Think about it.

Every major reality competition franchise is being made into an expert version, so we've come up with one for *The Amazing Race*. Now you know why we are sitting in your office, you know why I spent months chasing down talent deals and thousands of dollars creating material. I've got a *reason for being* in that office with that network at that moment.

Now the buyer knows the purpose of what's to come and is

ready to hear and understand the story. I just told the buyer that Bambi is a little deer and his mother just died and he's all alone and must survive in the forest. Now here is his story.

Identify your reason for being and create the intro that puts your audience in the right place and the right frame of mind.

Start with what your audience wants out of your proposal, then look for the story that explains how you discovered how to deliver it to them.

That's how you use an opening.

THE CALLBACK

Now that you have a reason for being, you want to be able to get as much leverage out of it as possible. If your reason for being is strong and compelling, you want to reinforce it if you can.

In the structure of your 3-Minute pitch there is a perfect opportunity to do so.

The callback is one of the most-used devices in comedy. Because it's meant to drive laughs, it's very deliberate and obvious. If you've ever seen a stand-up comedian, you'll see this over and over. He or she will establish a story and a joke early and then throughout the set will hark back to that joke. It's always good for a laugh and keeps the momentum going.

You can't see it as clearly in film or TV storytelling because it's designed to be subtle. In a murder mystery it will be the clue—the empty milk bottle—you don't recognize at first but will become relevant later. In a romantic comedy it's the moment when the couple realizes something happened earlier—a chance meeting on the subway—that was the true signal they were falling in love.

The idea of the callback in a pitch is to repeat your reason for being and verify it. It's metaphorically the moment you say, "See what I'm talking about!"

It's a great way to connect your pitch to the opportunity you're presenting. It brings your audience a step closer. It tells them, "Now you see it, too, don't you?"

The way we've set up your 3-Minute pitch lends itself perfectly to this callback. It fits naturally after you establish your edge, which is that thing that made you realize how good it really was, that thing that you just have to listen to. Once you've stated your edge, you'll feel that natural moment to say, "Aha, now you get it." So you want to layer in that verification as your callback.

For example, when we were pitching *Bar Rescue*, my opening was about how big personality and expertise were the benchmark of cable TV franchises and that for the audience to buy in to the over-the-top personality, there needed to be real depth. There needed to be substance, or the audience would smell the fake a mile away. I talked about how Gordon Ramsay was known for his combative style and rants, but he had the goods to back it up. He is *that* good of a chef. Simon Cowell was mean, but he was *always* right. If you don't have the goods, you're dead in the water. When I met Jon Taffer, it was obvious within minutes that he had the goods.

It's perfectly clear in my opening. I establish that I'm there because I found a talent with a huge personality who also has the knowledge and depth to back it up. (Just a reminder: when building your opening, make sure you don't use big gestures and make grand statements. I was careful not to say Jon would be the next Gordon Ramsay, and I didn't say he was going to be a huge TV star. I said the big boys get away with big, aggressive personalities because of their backgrounds. Jon has the background.)

So now if we go back to the *Bar Rescue* pitch, after the opening, I laid out the hook of the show and then the edge (the Butt Funnel—how could you forget the Butt Funnel?). After the Butt Funnel explanation, it was the perfect time to call back to my reason for being. "You see, when Jon pulled out a blueprint of a bar he was designing and showed me how he used the Butt Funnel, I knew there was so much more to him than just the big personality. Jon knows as much about bars as Gordon does about restaurants."

Can you see how that dovetails perfectly? That's how you use a callback. I reinforced that Jon is an expert with serious knowledge, which is what I was saying in the opening. Crucial here is that I didn't say it straight out at the beginning. I let the facts and the information do the work. I didn't have to state it and then prove it. I informed them and then led them to that conclusion.

Take your opening reason for being and ask yourself, "When did I realize I was right?" Is there a story or a moment that verified all your thoughts and assumptions about your proposal? What happened that made you realize what you were thinking was true?

You've built an opening that says how you came to be. Now build your callback as the part where you knew that was right. Something must have given you that validation.

This will take your audience on the journey you went through as you became committed to your project. You want your audience to walk through your rationalization story the way you did. Your journey is a story. It's a story of your commitment and purpose.

How did you get there? Something happened that led you to be involved, and now you are sharing it with others. Your pitch is a story that says, "Here is how I came to believe in this." Remember. If they can see your business, product, or service the way you do, they'll have to be interested.

So how do you get them to see things the way you see them?

First you explain the reason you got involved or excited (opening), then tell the story of what it is (what) and how it works (how), and then explain how you knew you were on the right path (Are you sure?). Then you talk about your biggest struggle (All is lost), then explain how you overcame it and the result (your hook), and share how amazing that feeling is (the edge) and how it was all leading you here the entire time (the callback) so now you can share this with others (Can you do it?).

Opening
What is it?
How does it work?
Are you sure?

All is lost

The hook

The edge

The callback

Can you do it?

You've built the story. You have your best three minutes.

BUT, BRANT, WHAT ABOUT THE ENDING?

That's the question I get every time. "How do I end it?" And after we've gone through all this detail and clever reconstruction and nuanced positioning of the pitch elements, everyone is expecting something that hits a crescendo of epic proportion to finalize and ignite the finale.

Yes! It's time for that flurry that is the end of the Fourth of July fireworks show! Get ready for the clashing of symbols and blaring of horns at the end of the symphony. Everybody dying at the end of a Shakespeare tragedy.

What is the ending of the 3-Minute pitch? How do I go out with a bang?!

Are you ready for it?

You don't.

You don't need an ending. You don't even want one.

After all we've put into the pitch, the ending has virtually no consequence. (I do love this part.)

Simply put, if you've laid out your pitch or presentation the way we've gone through it in this book, the way you end it doesn't make any difference.

I used to end my pitches with a clever saying or pun that led me back to my title. "And that's why *Run for the Money* will be a *run*-away hit!" or something equally cringe-worthy. But more and more I started to feel that cringe in the room. It was a virtual eye roll.

Everything up to that point was so natural and genuine that this forced ending started to feel more and more contrived and rehearsed.

So just stop talking. You've said enough.

If you've ever seen *Shark Tank*, you know that there is always an entrepreneur who says something like "So come on, Sharks, which one of you wants to take the plunge with us?" and you hear the groans and forced chuckles from the panel. It always feels like the contestants had momentum when they were talking about their business and their company, and then they snapped everyone back to "Oh yeah, I'm an amateur pitching you on a TV show."

You never want to say or do anything in your pitch that reminds the audience that they are being pitched or sold to. You don't want to remind them that you rehearsed this one thousand times and are making this exact same pitch to anyone who will listen. If you are telling a story and leading them with your bread crumbs of information, you are building momentum and focusing their attention. Your catchy closing line or pun isn't the climax of the pitch—you've already been there—so don't try to make some clever wordplay the finale.

I've experimented with dozens of different closing techniques, and nothing worked when I deliberately tried to come up with something to be an ending.

Eventually I discovered the one version that worked the best. It was basically nothing. Almost no ending at all.

This is about your *first* three minutes; there is always more to come and more to talk about. You don't need to try to wrap everything up with a bow.

In fact, when I pitch a TV show using a Prezi or Power-Point (keep reading for a crucial chapter coming up next), I end by simply showing the original logo slide and effectively say nothing. I actually mean that sometimes I literally say nothing. I just stop talking and show the logo.

It goes back to the very core of my principle Say Less and Get More. I had already explained the show, how it worked, and why it was so good, and proved that I could do it. What else of value was there left to say? Nothing. The pitch was done. Now it's time to engage and discuss. Any questions?

This works no matter the situation. Anytime you are going to be pitching and presenting, you will be faced with one of two different formats:

1. Pitch and engage—where you make your presentation to a single person or group and then discuss directly.

2. Pitch and present—where you will be speaking longer and without stopping to answer specific questions at the three-minute mark. This is very common in company presentations or large groups.

Ending without an ending works perfectly in both scenarios. The key is to have separation between the pitch phase and the engagement phase. After you finish your pitch but before questions or discussion, pause for a couple of seconds. It's like the commercial after the football game and before the postgame analysis.

"OK, now that you know what it is and how and why it works, I'll answer any questions you might have and share some other details you might be interested in."

I worked with a really funny CEO of an online betting site that was trying to take on established industry giants DraftKings and FanDuel. He was a really energetic and entertaining guy, and he just couldn't help but crack jokes and try to be clever in his presentation.

Some of it worked, but it came off as light and dismissive. He ran a public company and as such he had an additional layer of protocol to deal with when presenting. So when we had perfected his 3-Minute pitch, I told him to just end with the company logo.

"But we're not done. I have all this other information I have to go over," he said.

"I know, but having this clear break after your core pitch will be a signal that now you're going to get deeper into the details."

And that's how he did it. In fact, nearly every public company I work with follows this structure. You want to send the signal to the audience that it's time for questions and answers, even if they aren't actually asking questions. You are going to start giving answers to the questions they would most likely have. Or you're going to fill them in on some other interesting items that, once they understand the concept fully, will be infinitely more interesting and valuable.

Every one of those value statements you cut from your 3-Minute team is getting called up to the majors now.

What you'll find is that if you just stop talking after your pitch is done, you'll get the most informative and important interaction of your presentation in those next fifteen seconds. The first thing that comes out of your audience's mouths will tell you everything you need to know.

Pay close attention to those first moments. That's the good stuff.

You've got it! You've got your first, best, and most powerful three minutes. You have mastered the foolproof 3-Minute Rule, and now you are ready to unleash it on the world!

Let's just take a breath.

I hate PowerPoint.

Steve Jobs said, "People who know what they're talking about don't need PowerPoint." I know you know what you are talking about, and that you are most likely going to use Power-Point or some other program to deliver your pitch or presentation. You don't need it, but if you're going to use it, you'd better make sure you use it right.

The last thing I want is for all our hard work to be undone by PowerPoint. Believe me, it happens *way* more than it should.

CHAPTER 13

POWERPOINT-LESS

I may not have met you or know anything about you, but I'm guessing you are probably just as annoyed and put off by PowerPoint as I am. Actually, I'm not sure that's possible. I really hate PowerPoint.

And excuse me for being presumptuous, but there is a good chance that if you use PowerPoint or Prezi or some other software, you are part of the problem.

It's not your fault. It's just that nobody laid any ground rules or guidelines that we could all follow so we don't drive each other crazy with awful PowerPoint presentations.

So we're all to blame. (Yep, I've done it too.)

If I had to guess, either you've literally read off the stuff that's on the slides, which your audience has already read, or you've left the presentation up on the screen for them to read instead of listening to you. And I'm almost positive you've used your slides as your handouts.

Stop doing this!

When I explain how to use PowerPoint in a seminar or

keynote, I always ask, "Is anyone here a graphic designer? Is anyone selling their ability to make cool graphics or presentations?"

Nobody ever (well, once) raises their hand.

"Then you do not need to focus on your presentation graphics or slides."

If you've ever seen me present or speak onstage, you know I use simple black-and-white text slides for all my presentations. Literally. I have a team of some of the greatest graphics and animation experts in the world at my disposal and only use simple black-and-white text. Nothing more.

Why?

I use the slides to accentuate my information; I'm not looking for them to do the work for me. And I sure as hell don't want them distracting the audience.

Savvy and sophisticated audiences have seen all the tricks and infographics, whiteboards, and 3-D animated versions of pitches.

And as I've been saying for the entire book, *they just want the information*.

Don't get me wrong, making your slides or presentation look professional is a good idea. It does convey something about your company. But I've never come across a company with a concise and compelling pitch that had cheap-looking or amateurish slides.

It's *always* the exact opposite. They get their slides all fancy and detailed and colorful and create cool transitions and flying bullet points but have all their information mangled and messy. *Always*.

I can't tell you how many pitch tapes I see loaded with

transitions and pushes and wipes throughout the whole thing. It just screams amateur. Bells and whistles now signal to the audience that you are trying to distract them.

That's not what you want.

That's why I hate PowerPoint. It is the single biggest killer of presentations ever. It's a menace to society.

It drives me crazy.

I found early in my coaching (detailed earlier in this book) that I'd have to spend almost as much time helping companies simplify their PowerPoint as I did simplifying their message!

What was this tractor beam–like hold that PowerPoint had on my clients (and me for a while)?

I used to spend weeks and thousands of dollars designing and building glorious PowerPoint presentations for every show I pitched. They were beautiful, but looking back, they were totally unnecessary and unhelpful.

While I was discovering the power of the 3-Minute Rule and developing my technique, I was finding that these beautifully designed, elaborate presentations were actually confusing to the message. It seemed that with every new pitch I was taking out a transition or deleting a zoom, and saying to the team, "Just put up the picture with the text, I don't need it to move or dance."

This PowerPoint simplification process progressed hand in hand with my other pitch and presentation techniques.

I eventually developed a guideline I could implement quickly to help other people get their PowerPoints under control and on the right track. I just felt compelled to do something to help stop the spread of bad PowerPoint etiquette.

One day Hall of Fame speaker Jeffrey Hayzlett and I were on a panel together and I was voicing my displeasure of Power-Point and how it's misused, and Jeffrey said to me, "Moses only needed two tablets and ten bullet points to move his people, do you really need more?"

Boom. So true.

So now I call these my PowerPoint Commandments, and I have ten of them to really bring home the metaphor.

If you are going to pitch with PowerPoint, you should follow these commandments like I appeared to you in a vision and your book suddenly caught on fire.

Got it?

THE POWERPOINT COMMANDMENTS

YOUR HANDOUTS ARE *NOT* YOUR PRESENTATION SLIDES

If I could have people read and follow only one sentence in this entire book, I think this would be it: Your handouts are *not* your presentation slides. It would save the world so much aggravation. Without question this is the most common error I see across the board. When you have a handout or a "leave behind," it serves a very specific purpose. They are meant to be handed out and left behind *after* you've presented.

They are usually detailed and purposeful with a ton of information. That's great. I love a thick, detailed, glossy handout after everything is done. The problem is when you use those pretty pages as your slides and speak them. It's a bad look and it's bad form. Graphs and data slides don't help anyone if they need to be read to be understood. And if you are putting up slides that people can't read and talking about the stuff that's too small to see, you are just wasting screen space and opportunity.

You don't want to compete for attention with your own information.

People will read ahead if you give them something to read Whatever you do, don't give them something to read while you are talking. It's that simple. If you want to put a slide up to illustrate some work or test or something, remove all the text other than the headings and the conclusion. You can explain directly how the chart works and the parameters. That's why you're there in the first place. You only want to use those slides to guide your audience to important elements you are about to reveal.

This is so important I'm going to say it again: Never give people things to read during your presentation. People will always read ahead. Always. It will be distracting and unnerving, and all the work we've just done on flow and timing and structure gets tossed away. If you have big beautiful handouts, the best thing to do is to hold up your cool handout and say, "I'll leave this with you to go through after we're done."

Make different slides for your PowerPoint and your handouts. Your presentation is there to help you; your handouts are there to reinforce what you've already said. Important rule.

USE ANIMATION, TRANSITIONS, AND
FONTS SPARINGLY

In a world of instant communications and ubiquitous social media, cool transitions and flying animations are not impressive. Everyone has seen them before. Nobody is impressed or dazzled.

If they aren't impressive, what purpose do they serve? Does a flying or dissolving bullet point help deliver your message? Not really. So use them sparingly. I rarely if ever use transitions between slides or animate my text beyond having it appear when I click. Like I said before, bells and whistles don't excite an audience; they more often than not signal that you are trying too hard. And that's if you use them right. If you overuse them or use really different or strange moves, it's very distracting.

The same goes for fancy or multiple fonts. There is a reason that every major brand in the world uses simple, clean fonts in everything they do. Fancy fonts don't say anything other than you are just *trying* to be fancy. I strongly recommend using only one font in your PowerPoint, two at the most. Overfonting is something that's easy to do these days because PowerPoint has so many nifty fonts in that drop-down menu.

It's a trap, trying to make you look foolish. Don't fall for it.

I know when I see a sales tape or presentation with a bunch of graphic moves and cross-fades or cursive fonts that I'm probably dealing with an amateur. Don't send that signal.

SLIDES AND BULLET POINTS FOR CRUCIAL
OR KEY ELEMENTS ONLY

You don't need a slide or a bullet point for every single thing you say. This is another extremely common mistake, and to be honest I still get this one wrong myself sometimes. I will catch myself in a pitch building a bullet point or slide for too many points or thoughts. I have to go back and ask myself, "Does this move the story?" This is a writing term that challenges writers to justify every scene in a script. The idea is that a writer will often get in their own head and write scenes that build character or tension or are really cool but don't actually move the story along.

The rule is simple: If you don't need it, you don't need it.

You only need to make slides and bullet points for thoughts or statements that really need to be seen. You need to have a reason for each slide and each thing you put on the screen.

MAXIMUM OF 6 SINGLE-SENTENCE
BULLET POINTS PER SLIDE

Don't fill up your slide with text and lists. There is no point in listing fourteen different things on the same slide. You will be drawing the attention to your slides as you list things off, and that part of your presentation will become about a list on a screen.

Don't use more than six points on a slide. Keep it clean and the thoughts connected. If you are moving on to a different thought or section, move to a new slide. It's important that your slides don't force the audience to read through items. You need these bullet points to accentuate your talking points, not to make the points for you. So if you can, always have the bullet points come up on the screen one by one as you say them. If you put up a list of points and then try to talk through them, people will read ahead.

You don't need full sentences. You don't need to be grammatically correct in a bullet point. It's not meant to be read in the literal sense. When I make a bullet point list to pitch a show, I always try to keep the point to just one line.

- Full sentence not important
- Clear and simple
- Accentuate point, not make it
- You drive, not PowerPoint
- Audience will follow
- Message delivered

Do these look like the Post-it notes I've been talking about throughout this entire book?

Yep.

MAXIMUM OF 10 SLIDES

If you follow the first four commandments, this should be natural. However, it's most likely that you still are clinging to a few slides and ideas that you think need a slide but don't. The guide is a maximum of ten slides for your 3-Minute pitch or presentation. Anything more than that and you're giving a slide show and not a presentation. Follow the breakdown on pages 197–99 and keep it to ten.

After your three minutes you may have a little or a lot more to cover with your audience. I try to keep to a one-slide-per-minute guideline if I'm doing a keynote or longer presentation.

DON'T READ YOUR SLIDES

Every presentation or speech coach will give you this advice and command:

Don't read your slides.

You shouldn't read your slides. But let me expand this just a little because I have encountered a lot of people who can't memorize their 3-Minute presentation. In fact, I pitch so many TV shows that sometimes I don't have it perfectly memorized. So when I say don't read your slides, I'm not saying you need to have everything memorized perfectly. It's a nice touch, but it's not crucial. Ideally, if you are following the commandments, your slides are going to be brief enough that you won't need to read them. Use them as notes. It's helpful when a bullet point or a picture comes up that reminds you of the point you are making.

I use this technique in many of my speeches because I find it draws the audience to my point. Often I will pause slightly, turn to the screen, and click up my next slide or bullet point. Then I'll read it and explain the context. Because my slides and bullets are so brief, this acts as a natural bread crumb trail. I'm using it as an attention-directing technique.

I'm directing the audience where to look and guiding them to what's next.

Don't read your slides, but anything you do read should be used to bring your audience to each point in the pace and order you've decided.

A PICTURE IS WORTH 1,000 BULLET POINTS

I've seen some of the most dynamic and interesting presentations given without a single piece of text on the screen. If you can use a photo and speak to it, you will do better than if you have a bunch of tiny written text. It's better to just put a picture of your warehouse and describe it than to use bullet points with the dimensions and a list of facilities.

People process visual images almost instantly, so they will be refocused on your words seconds after they see an image. You can push ideas through imagery far better than through text. If you have the image, the text isn't needed.

Having said that, the same rules apply for simplicity and relevance. You don't want to use thirty pictures in your first three minutes. You don't want a picture for every bullet point either. One picture should take all or most of your bullets for that slide. A picture should be used as a powerful image and not a space filler.

DON'T BE AFRAID OF WHITE SPACE

You don't need something on the screen every second of your presentation. In a keynote, I will often use a generic logo or blank screen for several minutes at a time. Again, I tell the audience where to look and what to focus on. I do that every second of the presentation. The audience doesn't have the time or the inclination or the opportunity to look at something or read something that I don't want them to. If I'm not speaking directly to the text or image on the screen, I don't have anything on the screen. This directs the audience to focus on me when I'm talking and focus on the screen when I put something up there. It makes it all more deliberate and focused. An audience naturally wants to be led through your presentation.

So use blank space to your advantage. If you find areas where pictures or words are not needed, then put up your logo or go blank. You'll find that the slide that comes up after those spaces really jumps out. Use that moment.

PACE YOURSELF

When you use PowerPoint, it may make you speak faster. It may not be obvious at first, but trust me, it does. It makes you feel like you have to "get somewhere," so you start down a path. You feel rushed because you have a forthcoming slide you need to get to.

It's a great exercise to time your presentation without your PowerPoint and then time it again with the slides. You should be about 10 percent to 15 percent *longer* with your slides. If you are using the slides correctly, they will be part of your pitch and you'll interact with them a little.

If you find you are faster with your slides, then you need to find the elements in the slides that you are skipping over. You will probably find bullet points that need space. Most often I find clients have bullet-pointed a thought that actually needs to be explained or has some gravitas to it, but because they see it as a simplified bullet point, they gloss over it more when they use the slides.

Remember to work from your pitch to your PowerPoint, not the other way around. Don't let that PowerPoint lead you or dictate your language or pace.

PEOPLE WHO KNOW WHAT THEY'RE TALKING ABOUT DON'T NEED POWERPOINT

Steve Jobs might have said that, but my dad was a career salesman who followed this philosophy before PowerPoint was even invented. Your PowerPoint has to be a bonus and not a crutch. Too many people use it as a way to tell their story or convey their information, and that's hard to do well. There are CEOs all over the world banning PowerPoint presentations from their meetings. Why? Because PowerPoint when used as a crutch is simply repetitive and unpleasant. Nobody wants to sit through another PowerPoint presentation. What they want is your information delivered as efficiently and effectively as possible. The key is to only use PowerPoint if it helps you do that.

Honestly, more times than not, I don't even use PowerPoint anymore. I'll bring in a copy of the book, or one piece of tape, or the article that inspired the idea. I can convey the idea so clearly and effectively now that most times the PowerPoint feels like it's taking up space. I use it when it really helps me or I need to illustrate several specifics.

YOUR 3 MINUTES AND POWERPOINT

Now that you have those commandments down, I want you to go back through and read them again. I'll wait. It's that important.

To this day I have never had a client or anyone get their PowerPoint simplified enough in their first try. It's always like working with a director on a movie. They are so invested in every scene, it's like telling them to cut one of their children out of their will.

I have had to go through just as much work to get some people to understand the value of simplifying their Power-Point as I did trying to get them to simplify their message.

So read the commandments again.

Now that you're on board with that, let's look at how you might build a PowerPoint to fit with your 3-Minute pitch.

In building the pitch we've taken everything of value about your business, product, or service and brought it front and center. You are already dealing with the best of the best. This is the all-star team of information.

Let's use PowerPoint to your advantage. Use it to accentuate and highlight the most valuable points and drive them home. Your PowerPoint is your wingman. It's the Scottie Pippen to your Michael Jordan, the Mr. Spock to your Captain Kirk. You can be greater together!

First let me give you the outline to work from:

Opening = 1 slide—The fact or image that gave you the reason for being. Show or tell them how you got here.

What is it? = 2 slides—Your logline or first sentence that explains it best should be its own slide. "Freebird is the app that lets bars, restaurants, and nightclubs pay for clients' Uber and Lyft rides" is a slide with just that. The next slide can be three or four other clear points.

How does it work? = 2 slides—This is where you put a few clear bullet points. If you are describing functionality, a list works perfectly here.

Are you sure? = 1 slide—This is usually a simple list. You don't need to put up slides of graphs with crazy detail about your numbers. You just need to put up the graph and speak to it. If the audience is interested, they'll get to your proof later and dig in.

All is lost = 1 slide (optional)—If you have a good negative to bring up, having it on a slide will help transition it. It shows you've addressed it and have the confidence and plan to overcome it.

The hook = 1 slide—One simple slide that highlights and summarizes that one thing that ties it all together.

The edge = 1 slide—I always try to have a picture here that illustrates that push-it-over-the-edge moment. In my *Bar Rescue* pitch, I had a slide of the blueprint of the bar Jon was designing with a big arrow pointing to the Butt Funnel.

The callback = 0 slides—It is tempting to put your see-I-told-you moment on a slide, but you need to resist. This moment is intended to feel like it's happening in real time. Like you just heard yourself pitching it and can't help but say, "You see what I mean?" If you have a slide here it will lose the spontaneity and feel like part of a sell.

Can you do it? = 1 slide (optional)—If you know your audience or they know you or the details of the action items are kind of obvious, you really don't need to have a slide here. You can easily talk it through and you are done. When I pitch a TV show, I never have a slide about how I'll actually produce it unless there is something very unique or special. If there is, it probably moves up to the "Are you sure?" section.

Every TV buyer knows me. They know I can produce and how my production will work. Sometimes I talk about the budget if I want them to know that we can do the show for a reasonable price, but I wouldn't put a slide up that says "Less than $700,000 per episode." That's not needed. I can just say it.

That's the outline of a solid 3-Minute pitch or presentation. No more than ten slides. Each slide is helping you drive home the message. Each slide adds something.

Just take a step back and think for a minute. I'm sure you've been pitched many things in your life by someone using PowerPoint. Imagine if every time you saw someone's PowerPoint presentation it was only ten slides, with simple bullet points and pictures. Honestly, how much better would the world be if we all followed these guidelines?

THE DAD TEST

My dad was a sales professional all his life. I suspect that's where I learned many of the things that have helped me along the way. He was working with a pharmaceutical company in the dental industry that required him to travel and pitch insurance companies on covering a new treatment. The idea was, you pay for this treatment for all your clients and you'll spend less on dental claims. The pitch was a little complicated because it involved some medical jargon and some serious dental knowledge to grasp how this treatment worked. If you understood that, you could then extrapolate the cost savings.

My dad flew to Toronto to meet with one of the largest insurers in the industry. He rented a car and stopped for a bite to eat before checking into his hotel. While he was having breakfast, his car was broken into and all his luggage, including his presentation material, was stolen. Yikes.

This was years before PowerPoint was invented, so all my dad's presentations were done with actual slides and a projector. Also, this wasn't an "email me the files and I'll print them at FedEx" situation. Email hadn't been invented. This was a "you have a 3:00 p.m. meeting and you have nothing and no way of getting your hands on your material" situation.

My dad had no choice but to take the meeting, armed with nothing. He didn't even have a suit; he was still in his traveling clothes.

He entered the conference room and explained the situation to the group of eight executives and apologized, but it was what it was. He went ahead and explained the company and the treatment and how it worked. He didn't have any clinical trial graphs or chemical compound graphics to speak directly to, so he summarized as best he could. He stuck to the results and to the important details he knew by heart. The executives didn't have any papers in front of them to flip through or read ahead; they just listened. They made eye contact.

You see where this is going.

By the time his pitch had ended, the executives were engaged. There was a lot of "I'd like to see that" and "Please send me those details," but it was clearly a more positive result than he was used to at such a meeting.

My dad was stunned by this reaction. He was literally sweating and near panic when he realized he was going into this meeting with nothing, but he was feeling ten feet tall and bulletproof coming out. He often said it was one of the best pitches in his career.

He started distributing his pitch handouts *after* his presentation from then on (but he always wore a suit) so he could just have that connected pitch before the audience dove into the material.

This is a good test. If you pitch your three minutes cleanly without any visual or PowerPoint help, you have to be perfectly comfortable with that *and* it has to stand on its own.

If you've gone through the steps in the book, you should be feeling confident. That's the easy part.

Look at your PowerPoint. Does it do your pitch justice? Is your pitch noticeably better with the PowerPoint? Work until you find that you are better with the slides and the images are helping you. You'll know right away when you find that sweet spot.

If you go to 3minuterule.com/powerpoint, I've uploaded a few of my TV pitches so you can see how simplified and clean

I make my presentations. Also, don't forget to check out the Freebird investor deck.

When you think you've got it down, send me your Power-Point slides and I'll give you a grade on simplicity and clarity.

You are done! Now it's time to close the deal, right?

Wrong.

CHAPTER 14

"ARE YOU PUTTING ON RED LIPSTICK?"

B rant, are you putting on red lipstick?" my mother asked me the other day, not at all suggesting I was cross-dressing.

She was referring to a presentation I was showing her that had a lot more graphic sizzle and showmanship than it had clearly presented information.

My mom always says, "The delivery isn't nearly as important as the message itself."

In today's world, using a multitude of tricks to close a sale rarely works if you don't have your pitch right. If you do have it right, you don't need tricks. Most of the techniques we've been taught about language and the sales process have been overwhelmed and smothered by the information age. In fact, there are a few common styles, actions, and "closing" techniques that will actually detract from the message.

It's one thing to have a personal style and delivery that

doesn't help you in a pitch or presentation. It's another thing if it's damaging you.

This final chapter represents my continuing mission to help eradicate this issue every time you pitch and present. Much like my war on PowerPoint, I'm relentless in my pursuit of simplicity and clarity.

If you've done everything right up to this point in crafting your presentation to release your absolute best and most powerful information, you've still got a great chance of screwing it up during the presentation itself. Let's see how to avoid this.

My crusade for simplicity and clarity began a decade ago, when I decided to start my transition from TV and film producer to coach and speaker.

I was running development for 3 Ball Productions. The television business was booming, and we were having an explosive run of sales. *The Restaurant* had done well on NBC, *The Apprentice* (yeah, that one) was doing well there too. *Ghost Hunters* and *American Choppers* were also huge hits.

All of these hit shows also had impressive ancillary businesses created around the shows. There were huge licensing deals and product lines and touring opportunities that were well beyond the normal television production cycle. Everyone was cashing in, and we wanted to get in on the action too.

The Biggest Loser was our biggest hit show, and it was quickly becoming a marketing and merchandising dream, with diet plans and workout gear and dozens of other non-TV-related revenue streams flooding in.

We hired a head of business development to chase down as many opportunities as possible for every show we sold. His name was Kurt and he was damn good. Within the first few months he had gotten Walmart to come on board for *Extreme Makeover: Weight Loss Edition* products for big money. He was hungry, we were insatiable, and the market was ripe.

One day Kurt came to me and said, "I have something big I'm working on."

"Let's do it, I love big ideas, what is it?"

"We're going to look for the next superstar salesman, like *The Apprentice*, but for sales guys," he said excitedly.

He could see my lukewarm response. "Ugh, we've talked about that kind of thing. It's not exciting. People don't aspire to be salesmen."

"You're crazy," he snapped back. "Like 60 percent of the entire workforce is in sales. Everyone is selling something! The market is huge!"

"Well, I probably can't sell it." I was still frowning.

"But forget the TV part of it, that's the small part," he continued. "The money we can make on courses and systems and corporate training will make the TV show look like a snack. We could afford to pay the network to put the show on the air."

Now he had my attention.

"And I found the guy. *The* guy who can make it all happen." He grinned from ear to ear.

Kurt then explained that he had found a corporate sales trainer who was doing very well, was good-looking enough for TV, and was willing to cut us in on all the action.

"He becomes the host, training and judging twelve of the country's best salespeople and, like *The Apprentice,* each week we give the contestants a specific company and specific product to sell. Whoever sells the most wins!"

I filled in the rest. "Each week we bring on a new sponsor who wants to showcase their new product and have our guy teach the contestants how to sell it."

"Yes!" he exclaimed. "Xerox will pay a fortune to be in that episode because twelve contestants are devising the best ways to sell their new machine. But that's only half of it."

"There's more?" I was in.

"When a sponsor comes on board, they have to agree to hire our guy to train their entire sales department. It's part of the sponsor package. We will develop a line of instructional DVDs and coursework to sell as part of the package. It's a massive business opportunity."

I could see it. We went after it.

My team outlined the creative and the format of the show and got to work preparing material. Kurt and his team spent the time looking for sponsors and making some preliminary phone calls.

I knew the business idea was more compelling than the show idea. Even though we had really dug in creatively, I wasn't convinced we had a great stand-alone TV show. So I was excited to meet our sales talent to see if he could inspire more creative juice for the show.

A dozen of my staff assembled in the conference room when Dale (not his real name) joined us. He was just like he looked on his website, smiling and confident.

He began to go through the course he was teaching to sales professionals across the country. This was going to be the backbone of our TV and business idea.

He was awful.

He was so bad I wanted to stop him halfway through and

kick him out of the building. It was like a terrible stand-up routine mixed with the worst used-car-salesman advice and guidance.

He couldn't stop talking about "closing" and how to set up the room to dominate a customer. It was nauseating.

He talked about how he taught salespeople to scan a client's office for photos or clues as to what kind of interests and hobbies they might have. Then he instructed his students to make up similar hobbies to form a connection. He literally used an example of seeing a picture of his client holding a fish and how he made up a story about being a fisherman himself. He laughed hysterically as he explained that he never fished a day in his life. I guess he thought this was something to be proud of.

He even went through the "use your client's name, it's the sweetest sound" chestnut.

Needless to say, Dale was not our next TV star. When we did a little more digging, it turned out he hadn't even created the material he was using, he was just poaching it from other experts.

I was stunned to learn that there was that much bad information out there that he could recycle.

That was the moment that made me want to do what I do today.

I remember saying to Kurt after the meeting, "If I said or did any of the things he talked about, I'd get kicked out of every network meeting and never be allowed back."

Kurt was a bit chagrined. "Maybe you're the one that should be teaching people," he said.

It was the first time I thought that what I was doing could

possibly help people. And I knew damn well that I wanted to stop anyone from trying to connect with a potential client by making up a fishing story.

ALWAYS BE CLOSING

I've seen these words everywhere from pop culture to internet memes. I'd love to change the saying and the memes to be "Information closes itself," because that's what I believe needs to be spread.

We've seen that with today's information-saturated audiences, there is always the danger of undermining the quality of your information by pulling the focus to you personally. Dale's fish nonsense is one example.

In TV and movies and onstage, we call a direct outreach to the audience "breaking the fourth wall." It's the idea that an audience is immersed in your story and therefore ignores or forgets the fact that they are watching a TV show or film or play that was created for them. If you break that "wall," it pulls the audience out of the story and reminds them that they are *watching* something, not experiencing it.

Sometimes this is effective. *Deadpool* is a hugely successful franchise that uses this technique often, as Ryan Reynolds's character speaks directly to the camera. But they do it for laughs and it's integrated into the plot and the character. There are only a handful of shows that have even tried it, let alone used it successfully. Breaking the fourth wall is a risky proposition even when it's done right.

Here's the problem: Imagine if in the final scene of *Brave-*

heart (what else?) you saw the cameraman's dolly roll across the screen or the boom mic dropped into the frame. Or maybe you saw stagehands or the sets for the next scene in the background.

It would still be the exact same scene, with the same elements, but it wouldn't have the same impact.

Why does it matter if the sound equipment is visible?

Because it takes the audience out of the story, out of the moment, and out of the process, and it reminds them with a jolt that they are watching a movie. It pulls the focus to the creation of the story and away from the story itself. It interrupts what storytellers call the suspension of disbelief.

Filmmakers don't usually want that. They want the audience to be immersed in the characters and the story. They want the audience to experience the flow of the acts and the progress of the journey as it plays out through the conclusion.

The same goes for your pitch. You don't want to pull your audience out of the story and remind them they are being sold to.

Your pitch is a path of information to follow. It's vital to let that information take the lead. Often, too much emphasis on style and personality muddies the message. Stay out of your own way.

I struggled with this when I was starting out. I was always about the big personality of a high-energy presentation. Often my enthusiasm would overshadow what I was presenting, or worse, it would water down the authenticity of what I was saying.

Let's go back to the red lipstick and how my mother taught me the value of showmanship in small doses.

My mother is active in the international singing organization Sweet Adelines. It's a worldwide competitive choral group with twenty thousand members in twenty-four regions that span the globe. Each chapter of Sweet Adelines consists of up to 150 women who practice all year for their Super Bowl–style international final competition. This features thousands of women, sequined and choreographed onstage, singing barbershop harmony. If you've ever seen the movie *Pitch Perfect*, picture that, but for grown-ups and a whole lot bigger.

As I got older my mom became more involved with the organization as a whole. She went from chorus director to judge to judge trainer to international judge adjudicator to eventually president of the global organization. My mother speaks to, trains, and coaches choruses across the globe and sets the standard by which the judges are judged. I've heard her called the Wayne Gretzky of Sweet Adelines (Canada's unofficial highest nonmilitary honor).

Being a smart kid, I often turn to my mom for advice. She has great insight on the mind-set of guiding and coaching for excellence. Before I develop a new topic or subject for an audience, I run it by Mom first.

One of the most valuable pieces of advice my mom ever gave me was about presentation and showmanship on a personal level.

"Brant, that sounds like you're putting on red lipstick."

She is referring to the invariable instinct of a chorus to spruce up their look when they've hit a wall with their score and want to go to the next level.

"They look at their costumes, or their choreography, or

their makeup," Mom says. "When I tell them they need more resonance from their vocals, they don't want to hear it. That's a lot of work and it's hard for them to accept. Until they realize that it's about the sound, I can't really help them. Once their sound is at its absolute best, then the lipstick matters, the choreography counts, the sequins make them shine. Each and every year, the championship chorus is the one that sings the best, with the showmanship to set them apart."

I find the same thing many times when I'm coaching. Clients want me to tell them it's an easy fix. They want to hear the problem is the graphics, or their tie, or their confidence. It's easier to deal with that than their content or business idea.

I have to tell them it's the content, not the presentation. It's the message, not the messenger.

When my mom sees me trying to spice up elements of a presentation to overshadow the lack of clarity, she asks, "Are you putting on red lipstick?"

And she's right. When I struggle to make a point as clear as I see it, when I struggle to find the right way to illustrate my ideas, I lean on my personality and style to pull me through. And that's not when I'm at my best. So when I see myself doing that, I have to pull back and work just a little harder. Once I get the information and the story at its highest level, then I feel comfortable adding a little flair here and there.

So always look to your information first, and how you deliver it second.

THE PITFALLS OF PASSION

I hear this far too often: "Pitch with passion." I understand the idea and impact of passion for your business, product, or service, and I know that the idea of being passionate about your presentation or pitch is absolutely crucial in most people's minds.

I'm not going to argue against that, but what I am going to be very clear about is that passion is wildly powerful and intoxicating in a presentation, but it's also incredibly dangerous and easily misused. I tell my clients, "Passion is a tightrope razor's-edge walk you take in a presentation. The more often you use it, the smaller the edge and the harder the fall."

"Passion" is just a catchall word for enthusiasm, excitement, engagement, or intense belief. It's effectively the gauge we use when describing someone's level of excitement for something.

The downside is that the more excited or passionate you appear about your presentation, the more you make the presentation about you. This is where that fine line comes in. You want use that passion to accentuate and drive your story, but you don't want to overpower it.

There are two main danger zones to be aware of when pitching or presenting as it relates to you personally and what we are calling passion.

DANGER ZONE 1: PASSION TURNS TO PROMOTION

Everybody does this. By displaying enthusiasm for your business, product, or service, you can quickly cross over from passion to promotion. It's where you make the audience feel that you are more excited about making the "sale" than you are about your information or opportunity. It makes the audience feel you are eager to sell, not eager to share. It breaks the fourth wall and breaks the spell you've been casting.

Your passion should be directed at the information. It's important to note that passion is not a blanket you throw over every element of your presentation. Passion is a wave you use to come in with some force to emphasize key information, and then retreat, only to build up again later. This should be dictated by the information, not by the mere fact that you're pitching. Rather than in effect saying, "Gosh, I'm so excited to get you interested!" you're saying, "Gosh, this is such great information I'm sharing."

You need to be informational, not promotional.

When you become promotional, it almost immediately destroys your credibility. Your statements of fact and information begin to be questioned and doubted because your audience starts to believe that you will say anything to achieve your goal. Today's hypersensitive audience is easily triggered into rejecting that promotional push.

How do you avoid being promotional?

Confidence.

Not confidence in a personal way, but confidence in your information. The stronger you believe in the quality, effectiveness, and value of your information, the more likely you are to let that information stand on its own.

Let's say that I was trying to pitch you on allowing me to cater your next party. And my plan was to bring Gordon

Ramsay to be the head chef and personally attend the party and oversee the dinner.

With that information, would I need to sell you on it? Would I walk into that pitch with any doubts? Would I feel a need to sell you on how great the evening would be?

No. I would let the information do all the selling. I'd be confident enough to just let the facts stand on their own. It's Gordon Ramsay! Enough said.

If, on the other hand, I was planning on bringing a chef who had never cooked for me before and whom I had never met, I might be a little less confident in your buying in. I'd be feeling the need to sell and convince you. I'd have to get creative and probably have to exaggerate or make promises I wouldn't be sure would pan out.

You can see the difference in these extreme examples. The more you believe, the less selling you feel you need to do. Believe me, the audience can sense this from you. The more you sell, the less confident you appear, and the less likely they are to believe and trust you.

Trust that your pitch or presentation will lead your audience where you want them to go. Trust that your audience will come to the conclusion you want based on the information alone. You don't need to push or promote it. You don't need to oversell it.

This can be hard because our basic nature drives us to promote and sell when we really want or need something.

I have a poster in my office that reads:

The greater your desire to achieve your outcome, the more likely you will turn Passion to Promotion.

There is a boxcar's worth of PhD dissertations in philosophy behind the idea that desire breeds action.

It's not rocket science. The more you want something, the more you'll do to get it. That manifests itself in different and perhaps strange actions, depending on the subject of your desire.

In a pitch or presentation, the passion/promotion conundrum is about the words you use and the way you use them.

If you become promotional in a pitch or presentation, the audience will feel your yearning for the outcome. If you continue to display that, you will appear desperate. And desperation is the absolute last thing you want to convey.

When you become promotional, you try to:

Say it right

Say it enough

Say it loud

This is the process we as humans go through when we are desperate for others to see things the way we see them.

You can see this really clearly when you are operating on instinct, like when you are angry.

I want you to picture the last really intense fight you had with your spouse or significant other.

You probably heard yourself or them say things like this in the exchange:

"That's not what I said!"

"You've said that one hundred times!"

"Why are you yelling?!"

When you are angry and in a confrontation, you are desperate to have the other person see your side of the argument, and your base instincts take over.

You try to **say it right.** You feel that if the other person isn't seeing your side, you didn't phrase the information correctly. You try to say it again in a different fashion or different style. It's shocking when they don't "get it," because you feel it was so clear and you tried so hard to make it easy to understand.

In a pitch or presentation, this desperation is conveyed when you try to get cute or clever with your words and language. It feels like you are trying really hard to lead or push your audience with wordplay or tricks. This is why I caution people about the use of neuro-linguistics or communication techniques. They are a quick way to tell the audience you are really trying to "say it right."

Let your information do the talking for you. Don't let the audience feel you pushing them.

When you try to **say it enough,** you feel like the person may not have heard you, or didn't understand the impact you intended. So you say it again . . . and again.

You end up repeating yourself over and over. You'll notice the angrier or more enraged you become, the more you keep saying the same thing. It's because the most important and powerful statement in your mind is something that *must* be heard, and when you don't get the result you are hoping for, you say it again.

In a pitch or presentation this is common because you have information that you believe will deliver the message. You say it a few times to make sure it gets through.

Don't. It's important to believe enough in the effectiveness of your information to let it stand on its own. If you have to repeat it, they probably won't believe it.

When you try to **say it loud**, you are trying to ensure that your important and crucial facts are valued at the highest level. In a heated exchange, you end up raising your voice louder and louder because each time, the increased volume says, "Listen to *this* piece of information," and because in your mind, that's the piece of information that you desperately want them to hear in that moment. It will win your argument. But the argument continues to escalate because when what you're shouting doesn't have the intended effect, you must try again, louder.

In a pitch or presentation, this is done in words and style. You color your phrases or statements with "loud" adjectives to increase the volume. Ask yourself how many times you've used "revolutionary," "groundbreaking," or "incredible" to augment your information. Such words aren't really needed, but when you do say them, you're trying to say those things louder.

In screenwriting, this is called using the "LYs"—short for using too many adverbs. It's looked upon as an amateur's way of describing a scene. It's when the writer says the character "happily" accepted his invitation rather than using a description: "Her eyes opened wide as a smile formed, and she nodded her head in acceptance."

Using adverbs in screenwriting is lazy. In pitching or presenting it's promotional.

To avoid becoming promotional in your pitch or presentation, go back to the core of your simplified information. Let it do the work. Be passionate about the information. Be passionate and excited about the value of your offering. Let the audience feel your excitement grow the way theirs would grow if they had your information.

Let the information and the conclusions lead you there, not the other way around.

DANGER ZONE 2: UNJUSTIFIABLE PASSION

This is a screaming red flag that you should avoid at all costs. This is when your audience sees you passionate or excited about something that doesn't merit such a response.

This not only draws attention away from your information but also causes the audience to judge you and your values. Not in a good way. You don't want to be in that position.

Have you ever had someone you know rave about a movie and then when you see it, not only are you disappointed in the film, but you ask yourself, "How can anyone think this was good?" And good enough to recommend and be enthusiastic about? What does that do for your impression of their tastes? It's hard to undo this impression.

It's been thirty years since I raved about and told my parents to see *Diggstown* (James Woods, Louis Gossett Jr.), and they still won't take my recommendations for movies. (I stand by *Diggstown*.)

Why does political disagreement ruin friendships today? Unjustifiable passion. You can't imagine a justification to support the Republicans or the Democrats, whichever party you don't support. This makes the disagreement about the person. People will end friendships if the other person's passion is strong enough for something they can't justify. Nobody ends a friendship with an ambivalent political foe. It's only the most passionate ones that draw that kind of conflict.

That's how powerful and dangerous passion can be.

I get bad ideas and pitches for TV shows all the time. Actually, I'd say 98 percent of all the pitches I get from outside producers are not good enough ideas to become TV shows. Half of those are just simply bad ideas. It's par for the course in this industry.

But every once in while I get a producer who comes in to wildly, passionately pitch such a terrible idea that not only do I pass on it, I tell my assistant, "Make sure they never get in my office again."

I can't tell you how many development executives have interviewed for jobs and pitched an idea in the interview. The interview was going great, but now they've come straight out and effectively said, "Here, judge me based on an idea that I think is good enough to pitch you right now." More than one candidate I was considering made me say, "If you think that's a good idea, you're not right for this business."

Being passionate about subjective elements is dangerous. Your goal should not be to show excitement for your opinion. It's to be passionate for the facts.

I always tell my clients that if you can start the statement with "I think" or "This could," then it's an opinion and you don't want to add any hype to it. If you're talking about a result or a fact, that's what gets you excited.

With Freebird, the fact that we scan for the credit card charges and match them to the consumers' rides is something we could justly be excited about. It changed the entire development of the service. The idea that Kurt thinks this "could" change the way advertising and marketing relates to transportation is an opinion and a conclusion, and that doesn't need flair or emphasis. In fact, I told him not to even say it.

The information will let the audience get there. He doesn't need to sell it.

Are you excited or passionate about an opinion or a conclusion? Are you trying to force that opinion or conclusion on your audience by selling it with your excitement?

Be confident in your information. Trust that your information and your three minutes will lead your audience to share your opinion and come to the right conclusion.

THE DIRECTOR'S CUT

As I mentioned in chapter 7, there is a reason that you never watch the director's cut of a movie and think that those missing scenes and extra thirty-two minutes of run time really helped.

You're not reading my final version of this book. You're reading the result of editors' and writers' notes and dozens of other people's input and adjustments on several drafts preparing for these final pages. This isn't a director's cut.

There is a reason that in almost every creative endeavor there is an evolved and purposeful notes process. Collaboration and outside influence almost always result in a better product. You can't be scared of, or dismiss, feedback from outside your circle. In an echo chamber you only hear yourself.

As my career progressed through television, I was continually given more and more autonomy over my creative choices. I was able to buy and develop any projects I wanted with little oversight.

I always pushed back on that. Why would I need it? It's a nice ego play, but I always felt that if I couldn't get my boss or their boss or the marketing department or the office PA to buy in to the pitch, what hope would I have to sell it and get it on TV?

Autonomy is most often a functional convenience, not necessarily a creative improvement.

So the final, and most important, piece of advice I will give you is that once you've done all the work of gathering and distilling and honing your information into the perfect three minutes, from Post-it notes to statements of value to finding your edge and your hook, *show it to other people.*

I know how frustrating it can be to ask people, "What do you think?" If you ask six different people, you will get eight different answers. People love to throw their opinions around. But it's worth the exercise. Show your presentation to people you think will like it and to people you think will hate it. The haters are often the most helpful. Let them punch holes in it so you can see where it's weakest.

You will become more confident in areas that you believe in and better prepared for flaws you would have overlooked.

You may be putting on red lipstick.

Once again, it comes down to the confidence you have in your information. Let it get out there and withstand some scrutiny.

As a final incentive, I urge you, as you review these chapters and build out your pitch or presentation, to reach out with questions or stories of success (or challenges) on the website

3minuterule.com. I love the momentum that's been growing around the Say Less and Get More campaign, and I'm inspired to follow others on their journey.

Please reach out and share your story.

I promise to read anything that's less than three minutes.

ACKNOWLEDGMENTS

Since I still haven't won an Oscar or an Emmy, I haven't gotten a chance to give my acceptance speech where I thank all those who've helped me get to where I am today. So I figure I'd better do it now. I'd start with thanking the United States of America for all this country has given me. Without the USA and all it stands for, none of this would be possible. And this goes beyond the book. Who I am today and all that I've done is possible because this country accepted and embraced me. I will forever be grateful to those who have served and sacrificed for these opportunities. I know freedom isn't free.

My wife, Juliana, for more than twenty-five years my single biggest supporter and partner. It was impossible to see where we are today from where we started. You still excite, challenge, and improve me. Thank you. My oldest son, Kahless, my only daughter, Briana, and my youngest son, Braden, you bring me joy and inspiration daily.

Thanks to my parents, Marcia and Dennis, who bestowed upon me some of my most favorable attributes and tolerated most of the unfavorable ones. They supported me in every way possible. To my brother, Shawn, my closest ally and most trusted adviser. You stood behind, beside, and before me in all my challenges and struggles on this journey. We're not done yet. Love you.

This book represents the culmination of a sometimes long and arduous journey to finally get where I'm meant to be. But it's also the beginning of another exciting chapter that I'm thrilled to start writing. So many key figures who have made it possible:

Wendy Keller, you are the book agent who made it all happen. I'm so happy I listened and followed your direction. That was a good decision. Jeffrey Hayzlett, for that dinner where I said, "I want to do what you do." You made me see another path and you've been a great friend and adviser. Phil Revzin, for making these words better and these thoughts clearer. My uncle Mark, for getting the ball rolling and providing the direct path. Wouldn't be here if not for NobleCon, and no question Channelchek is the future. Kaushik Viswanath, for that letter over the weekend that swayed me to Penguin Random House. I have no doubt this is the right home and you are the right partner. Well played.

David Foster. You gave me five thousand dollars the first day we met and said, "Don't take a deal because you need the money, you'll regret it." You let me stay at your home and you called my wife when I wanted to move to LA. You saw something and you believed. I wouldn't be here without you. Full stop.

Matt Walden. You led by example as a friend and as a mentor and I learned about who I wanted to be by watching you. I'll always be grateful for your guidance.

Sean Perry, my first agent and dear friend. You've always been in my corner and on my team. On our first day you told me that I had to make every pitch as good as that first one, because that's what I could be known for. I owe you for that.

Eric Benet, my best friend and brother. I have no idea how a black R&B singer and a white Canadian entrepreneur became soul brothers, but ours is not to ask why. Being listed in your album liner was one of my proudest moments, so I'm returning the love here.

Lorne Alcock, my oldest and closest friend. Hard to explain, and if you have to ask who Lorne is, you wouldn't understand the answer. You put this train in motion. You know the story better than anyone. You will always be one of my favorite people on this planet.

Life is a series of incidents, relationships, decisions, and actions that make up the path to where you are today. Some of those moments are significant the instant they happen, but for most of them, you have no idea how impactful they are till much later, looking back. And the people in these moments may never know the effect they had on the course of your life. It is such an honor to have the opportunity to look back at my journey through the lens of good fortune and try to acknowledge many of those people and moments that led me to this day. Again, it's more than just a book.

My very first business partner, Jag Phagura, for the JAM. Wow, what a start. My first mentor and inspiration, Eli Pasquale, you taught me to shoot for the stars, 'cause if you miss you'll still land on the moon. Pete Bodman and Trevor Timmerman, for Cage Taylor; not sure how any of this happens without those days. Norm Kilarski, for pushing like crazy and reaching out to David. Can't thank you enough for always being there. Joe and John from SHC, you guys supported me and were one of my first entrepreneurial inspirations way back in high school. Marinda Heshka, for always keeping it together. Cuauh Sanchez, for that Cancun connection; that was an absolutely pivotal moment. Dave Marsh and James Lemire, for the memories on the road. Kirk Shaw, for the help and tough love.

Scott LaStaiti, one of my first meetings in LA; who would have guessed we'd be here today, still friends and still working together. You've been a constant force for good in my life. Jason Heit, thanks for getting Scott to take that meeting. I owe you for that. Jeff Gaspin, for the offer and the support that lit the fuse; I still think of that moment. Lance Klein, for the parking-lot call at ABC telling Jeff Gaspin, "We have bigger plans for him." Ari Emanuel, for the "Is that the Canadian kid running around town?" phone call. McG and Stephanie Savage, for making that phone call. Mary Aloe, for stirring the pot and getting it boiling. The legend Dick Clark, for his offer, and Jimmy Miller, who told me not to take it. Matt Johnson and Skip Brittenham, for that boardroom meeting and for being my first lawyers. Michael Gruber, for taking a big chance on a kid who didn't know how little he knew. Gavin Reardon, for that MIP trip. Gary Benz, for putting me on the map in TV. John Ferriter, for the "but John isn't my agent" recommendation call. Angela Shapiro-Mathes, for the big opportunity; I hope you are as happy as I am about the way it all turned out.

J.D. Roth and Todd Nelson, for the life lessons. Kurt

Brendlinger, for being such an enthusiastic supporter; you inspire me. Reinout Oerlemans, for the exposure to the big leagues. Garret Greco, my right hand, still the gold standard. You will always be like family. Tracey Lentz, Mike Maddocks, and Ambrosio Avestruz, wow, what a run we had. Todd Weinstein, we've grown together and it's been a blessing having you in my corner personally and professionally. Josh Klein, you continue to make me better, and are one of the most creative people I know. Nate Taflove, for those early *Forbes* edits; you helped set the stage. Christian Robinson, projects together for fifteen years, from TV to lake play. You are the best. Aaron Marion, for the PR push, and Tanya Klich, for giving me the platform.

Hank Cohen, for being an amazing friend and supporter. Ever since we sold that spaceship to Fox, you've been my rock. Can't thank you enough on so many levels. Dean Shull and Jake Pentland, for the edits; Sean Reilly, for the validation; and Elycia Rubin, for the connections.

This book is a product of the skills I developed producing in Hollywood, but that all stems from the life and business lessons I learned from some amazing friends who influenced me through the years.

Mark Murr, for always being my go-to. George Salvador, the OG hustler making business happen before we knew what that meant. Ellen Gallacher, for that almost website business. Mark Koops, for the sunny British outlook on life and for taking care of me after I got fired; I'll never forget that. Rabih Gholam, for all those morning calls. Joel Zimmer, from the Malibu days to the present day. SallyAnn Salsano, for showing me another level of intensity, I absolutely love it. Jayson

Dinsmore, Aaron Rothman, and Eli Frankel, we were the Four Horsemen, what a bold move we almost pulled off. Geoff Kyle, Al McBeth, Morgan Gonzalez, and Keith Allen, for keeping me outside the Hollywood mentality. Paraag Marathe, I deeply appreciate our friendship, thanks for everything. Beth Stern, you are my animal rescue inspiration. Jeff Butler, you are a great friend and an incredible leader and businessman. My life has been better since you've been in it.

My extended family. Allan Pinvidic, you were the closest thing to a big brother. My aunts Margot and Dianne gave me a creative balance to our growing-up experience. My grandma Margaret, for always being the voice in my head. The Antonini clan—Marty, for planting that idea of playing music like that, and Cory, for that Fuddruckers clubhouse tutorial, among other things. Len, Kelly, Rob, Bonnie, Ed, and Deanie, for that "Dizzying" time. Ed, my wife will never forget that. Mike, for the house. Tony, for my mom; Christine, for being our mom away from home; and Louise, for being Louise. Brandon, for helping to put it back on the tracks as the wheels were coming off. Lui and Marie, for all you do and the example you set.

And finally, my cousin Tricia, the strongest, most resilient and inspiring woman I've ever known. God bless you, you give me the inspiration to seize the moment, to put my hand up when I'm scared, and to live better and be better today.

INDEX